This book is distributed as part of the Safe Children Project and is supported by individuals and businesses within the plain community.

Facilitating this project is Dove's Nest, an independent nonprofit organization that grew out of Mennonite Church USA in 2009. Dove's Nest equips faith communities with resources to keep all children and youth safe, provides educational trainings to social services in areas with plain communities, and offers phone consultations for those who need help or have questions about child/youth protection.

If you need help or have questions regarding the Safe Children Project, you may reach out to the regional crisis resources listed below:

Marlon Schrock	Mark Hochstetler	Leon B. Martin
Nappanee, IN	Sugarcreek, OH	Ephrata, PA
574-773-5405	330-852-3824	717-354-0680

To speak with a Dove's Nest consultant or co-author Jeanette Harder, please contact:
>Dove's Nest
>5723 North 99th Street
>Omaha, NE 68134
>Phone: 402-577-0866
>Email: Info@DovesNest.net

Consider suggesting that your local social services engage with Dove's Nest for training.

Additional crisis teams and resources are listed in the back of the book.

For the Sake of a Child

Allen Hoover & Dr. Jeanette Harder

Ridgeway Publishing
Stoneboro, PA

FOR THE SAKE OF A CHILD

*To obtain additional
copies please visit
your local bookstore
or contact:*

**Ridgeway Publishing
2080 McComb Road
Stoneboro, PA 16153
ph: (888) 822-7894
fax: (724) 376-2090**

*Cover Design: Ridgeway Publishing
Artwork: Samantha Becher*

ISBN 978-1-7330645-7-6

All Bible references are taken from the authorized King James Version unless otherwise noted.

Printed in the United States of America

Table of Contents

Foreword..vii

Introduction...xi

Chapter 1...1

Our Communities: Unique Strengths and Weaknesses

Chapter 2..17

Types of Child Abuse and Neglect

Chapter 3..29

Recognizing Abuse

Chapter 4..37

Positive Parenting

Chapter 5..47

Prevention of Abuse and Neglect

Chapter 6..61

Getting Help

Chapter 7..79

Role of Social Services

Chapter 8...87

Foster Care and Adoption

Appendix A..105

Recommended Books

Appendix B..107

Recommended Resources

About the Authors..111

Allen Hoover

Dr. Jeanette Harder

Foreword

The cold rain of abuse still falls on too many children among us.

Verbal. Physical. Sexual. Emotional. The abuse of neglect. Why?

Is it because many of us have listened to the words of Jesus, when He talks about millstones around necks as punishment for offending a child, in a language we fail to grasp?

Is it because our desperately wicked hearts, poisoned with human selfishness, have escaped transformation by the cleansing power of a genuine new birth? Is it because the outside of the cup receives undue attention while extortion and excess rage on the inside? Have we placed culturally correct behavior on a higher plane than the real thing?

Is it because too many of us live in the shadow of past abuse? Have too many of us stored the pain of childhood abuse in the dark, backroom of our hearts and dead-bolted the door with denial, lies, or fear of exposure?

No matter the reason, this generation must act. We must offer powerful solutions to help victims process past abuse. No band-aids. No quick fixes. No emotional shots in the arm that last only until the first rainy day.

We must look abuse in the eye and call a spade a spade. We're done tiptoeing around the feelings of a perpetrator or their families. We're done acting like all is well when abuse lurks, ready to pounce on yet another innocent victim. We're going to come out. Come clean. Come to the light. We will fear hiding more than we fear exposure. God calls this generation to renounce the hidden things of darkness with powerful pens, well-seasoned words, and the sword of the Spirit. God calls this generation to fight the abuse battle with renewed minds and transformed lives.

As I write this, the first day of 2019 dawns. Oh God, let it dawn to a brighter future for the victims among us. Let it dawn to renewed zeal. Give us answers. Give us the power to help. Give us the empathy to care.

Let it dawn to the day when abuse is only a memory with a red face. Let it be said that abuse is the way it used to be; but now, no more. No more dark dead-bolted rooms in the hearts of our dear youth. No more depression and anxiety oozing from the fearful; the lonely; the misunderstood; the hurting.

No more.

Oh God, let the day dawn when every child among us grows up with the sunshine of parental love, the security of protected purity, and the beautiful light of the glorious gospel of Jesus Christ flooding every room of every heart. Let the day dawn when the life-changing, heart-transforming gospel of Jesus Christ is preached every week. Everywhere. Let it dawn on leaders who blow the trumpet of righteousness that exceeds that of the Scribes and Pharisees; preachers who shine the light of the gospel of peace into every dark place in our community; not only in our community, but first in our community. Let leaders arise who burn agreements made with the devil, that age-old enemy of our souls; leaders who sign God's covenant with a pen dipped in the blood of sacrifice and resolve. Without reserve. Without thought of personal gain or fear of loss.

And then, oh God, when tough battles come, help us not to grow weary in well-doing. When those battles are won, help us to raise holy hands in praise to Your Name.

The law of our land awoke us out of yawning apathy into hand-wringing uncertainty. Now, it's time to move to powerful resolve. The time is here to own the problem of abuse, to take full responsibility, and in the fear of God, move forward.

Resolve may begin in one human heart but it will move to hundreds. Then thousands. All joining hands to form a hedge of protection against abuse. Any abuse. All abuse. One abused child among us in the next hundred years is one too many.

For the sake of the great name of our Savior Jesus Christ. For the sake of a watching world. For the sake of our people. And yes, for the sake of a child. Let it be so.

"Now unto him that is able to keep you from falling, and to present you faultless before the presence of his glory with exceeding joy" (Jude 1:24).

Marvin Wengerd
1 January 2019

Introduction

Mary's[1] heart beat faster as Daddy turned their horse into the lane. Oh, how she loved going along to auctions. Already she could smell the aroma of the lunch stand, that mixture of hot dogs, French fries, sauerkraut... mmm. She could hear the chant of the auctioneer, the chatter of the children gathered at the candy stand, and the outburst of cheers and whistles from a large group out in the field where a corner ball game had started. The bright sun glinted off the puddles of water after the showers of last night. Going along with Daddy to a sale was a rare treat for ten-year-old Mary.

Dad looked over from where he was tying the horse. "Do you think you could use two dollars responsibly if I gave them to you?" he asked with a twinkle in his eye.

"Oh yes," she breathed. "And can I go out to the ball game

Most of the anecdotes used in this book are actual happenings, although names and details have been changed to protect the identity of individuals.

after I've looked at the candy stand?"

Daddy nodded. "I guess that will be okay. Just be careful."

Fifteen minutes later, with her jaws working on a hunk of bubble gum and her pockets filled with "goodies" to share with her little sister and brother at home, she decided to head out to the corner ball game.

On the way, though, she realized how muddy the path was as she slipped and almost fell.

"Hey," said a kind-sounding voice behind her, "Be careful there."

Mary turned around and peered at a smiling older boy.

"This path is just too muddy," he stated matter-of-factly. "Why don't we walk on the grass over by the barn."

How nice it is to leave this muddy pathway, Mary decided, as she followed him over toward the barn. The boy was so friendly and he told her his name was Daniel. He talked about the rainstorm last night, and how nice it was that the sun was finally shining again. Just when they were almost past the barn, Daniel pointed toward the door. "I wonder what is in there? Shall we go explore it?"

Mary looked up into Daniel's face. He was still smiling, but something just wasn't right. When he reached out as if to take her hand, she instinctively stepped back. She looked around and suddenly noticed there was no one else around at this end of the barn. An icy fear went through her heart, and she could almost hear her mother saying, "Always remember the three rules. One: Stay together; two: Don't go off the property; and three: Don't go with anyone, regardless how nice they seem."

Without a word, Mary turned and ran back toward the auction as fast as her legs could carry her, leaving Daniel *standing there staring after her in surprise.*

Mary found her father visiting with a group of men near the auctioneer. She went to him and just stood there. Finally, he noticed her and bent down to see what she wanted. In a rush, she told him what Daniel had said. Dad's face instantly changed from an expression of mild annoyance to alarmed concern.

"Can you show me this Daniel?" he asked.

She shrugged her shoulders, but went with him toward the barn. Suddenly she saw him again. "The boy with the blue jacket," she pointed as she spoke.

Mary stood and watched as Daddy strode across the field toward the boy. Even from where she stood, she could see how uncomfortable Daniel was as Daddy talked to him. Suddenly, Daniel turned and started walking out toward the road very fast, with Daddy close behind him. When Daniel reached the road, he jumped on his bike and pedaled swiftly away.

Daddy came back to Mary and squatted down beside her. "Are you okay?" he asked kindly. "What do you want to do now? Do you want to stay with me?"

Mary's lip trembled. "I want to go home," she whispered.

Daddy knelt there in indecision for a moment. Finally, he said resolutely, "Okay, we'll go home now."

That evening when the children were in bed, Mom and Dad discussed the happenings of the day. Daddy noted how happy and bubbly Mary had been on the way to the auction, but she just sat with nothing to say on the way home.

"Yes," said Mom, "I noticed that she just wanted to lie on the couch when she came home. I finally got her to tell me

all about it. After I assured her that she had done the right thing, and how glad we were that she had remembered our rules, she ran off to play and was her happy self again."

After a long silence, Daddy said quietly, "We'll never know what might have happened if we hadn't taught our children the three rules. How easy it would have been for her to innocently go with this Daniel. I wonder if our younger children would have remembered the rules like Mary did." He paused, then added, "I wish I had found out more about this Daniel before he left. What if this wasn't the only time he tried approaching little girls?"

We all know how precious our children are to us, and also how vulnerable they can be. God has entrusted them to our care, and more than anything we want to keep them safe. Yet we know that sometimes this is easier said than done. Children have a knack for getting themselves into the most precarious situations. They are curious and want to experience, taste, climb and jump off everything. It's especially challenging for those of us who have large families and therefore many other responsibilities. We tell ourselves that our close-knit church communities are the best place to raise children, and in many ways this is certainly true. Our faith should guide all aspects of our lives. We love our children, and want them to feel that love in the same way we feel God's love in our lives. God's love is certainly a model for how we should love our children.

This book will discuss different types of abuse and neglect, and how our families and communities are uniquely strong and safe, yet how they might also be vulnerable. We will look at those strengths and vulnerabilities, and suggest ways to keep our children safe.

communities. Our greatest strength can become our weakness.

Chapter 1

Our Communities: Unique Strengths and Weaknesses

There is a universal truth that has been in force since the fall of man in the Garden of Eden. "Our greatest strengths can become our greatest weaknesses." As we look back at history, this fact is brought out again and again. How many communities and families and individuals and even whole civilizations

---

Our strengths:
1. Raising our children the same from one generation to the next
2. Our forgiving attitude toward those who wrong us
3. Our shared family activities
4. Our close community structure
5. The headship order within the church and home
6. Proper child discipline

---

have fallen because they have allowed their strength to become their weakness? This can also be true for us today in our church communities. Our greatest strength can become our weakness.

1

Let us list a few of these strengths here. Likely you could think of others.

Raising our children the same from one generation to the next

One of the greatest strengths of the Plain[2] communities across the U.S. and Canada is the ability to raise our children in the nurture and admonition of the Lord. How do we learn how to do this? First and foremost, we learn this from the way our parents raised us. We may say our child training is based on the Bible and the teachings of our church, and this may be partly true. However, if we are completely honest, we will admit that the techniques of our parenting are usually very similar to the techniques our own parents used.

Is this good or bad?

In most cases this is good. Even though we recognize that our parents were not perfect, their way of rearing their children likely resulted in producing godly, up-building church and community members.

But what if our father or mother had a weakness they never overcame? What if the father never learned to control his temper, or the mother tried to control her children by nagging and making them feel guilty? What if a parent used unnecessarily harsh physical punishment? Can you guess how their children will tend to raise their own children?

It behooves all of us to consider carefully the traditions we pass

---

[2] Conservative Anabaptists

on to our children, and decide whether they are the best traditions to be passing on, or whether they could be harmful.

To illustrate this, let us look at a true story.

Simon and Nathan Miller were brothers, growing up in the same house with the same mother and father. They grew up in a large Amish community. They attended church with their parents, worked together on their family farm, attended the local one-room school, and, in general, grew up as normal members of their Plain culture.

But their father was one of those people who liked to have things done right, and tended to get upset if things were not done the way he thought they should be. When he punished, it was usually in anger, and that anger could be aroused by the smallest infraction. When he was upset, he would often say things that would make his boys feel worthless or inferior. Like his father before him, and perhaps his father's father, he had a hard time building a relationship with his children. Simon and Nathan grew up with the impression that fathers were harsh masters who were almost impossible to please. Because their father had an unpredictable temper, he was someone to fear rather than respect or love. As they matured, their consciences did not always bother them if they were disobedient. It was easy to justify themselves with the thought, "What difference does it make? I can't do anything right anyway."

Now, to be fair, their father had good points as well. It was not that he did not love his children at all. But he had never been taught how to show that love to them. In short, he raised his children as he had been raised.

As the boys grew up and had contact with other families, they discovered that not all fathers were as harsh as their father was. As normal teenagers, they came to resent this and became rebellious.

As time went on, Nathan learned to overlook his father's shortcomings and determined that if he ever had a family of his own, he would learn to express the love that his own father had seemingly been unable to express. When he married and had children of his own, he accepted the help of others, including his wife, and this cycle of bitterness was broken. Although Nathan was not a perfect father, his children were able to feel their father's love as they grew up.

Simon, on the other hand, became ever more resentful of his father. As the bitterness settled into his soul, he became more and more like his father, with an unpredictable temper and a resentful attitude toward anyone who tried to help him. As his own children grew up, the cycle was repeated, with several of them continuing on the path of rebellion and bitterness.

Our forgiving attitude toward those who wrong us

Forgiveness is such an integral part of our Christian walk of life. It is a command that Jesus gave to us, and which He himself practiced. He even prayed for those who nailed Him to the cross, "Father forgive them, for they know not what they do."[3]

A parent who lost a child in the Nickel Mines school shooting in 2006 recalled the time someone challenged him on forgiveness. "How would it be possible to forgive Charles Roberts?" he was asked. "To forgive so quickly is not realistically possible. It would

---

[3] Luke 23:34

not even be normal."

The answer was, "The decision to forgive was immediate. The actual emotion of forgiveness took a while longer. Even now, ten years later, I still need to work on it almost daily. However, I realized that if I did not forgive, if I allowed bitterness to enter my heart, I could end up being like Charles Roberts."

Yes, forgiveness is an important part of a Christian's life. Yet, just as Jesus loved the sinners, yet hated the sin, there are still times today when an abuser needs to be held accountable for his actions. If an alcoholic repented and made his sins right with God and the church, we would likely not allow him to eat his meals at the local tavern. We would want him to stay far away from all temptations and receive counseling and help to overcome his alcohol addiction. In the same way, a habitual abuser needs to be held accountable so that he or she can receive the treatment they need to break the iron grip of their addiction.

Without significant treatment, most offenders will continue their wrongdoing. Depending on the nature of the abuse, it may be legally required and necessary that the abuser be reported to the proper authorities to keep him or her from hurting more people. This does not mean that we do not forgive the abuser. It simply means that they need to be held accountable so that both the abuser and the abused can receive the proper help and the cycle can be stopped.

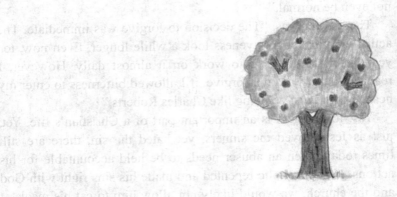

Our shared family activities

What better way to raise a family than working together, eating together, and worshipping together. The children learn responsibility at a young age. They gain a good work ethic and learn to know what is expected of them as they grow up. There is an old saying that in a family, "more is caught than taught." As children grow up, they will often look to their parents as their first role models. If there is a large family, the older ones learn to help care for the younger ones.

However, our times together on our farms or in our home businesses come with certain dangers, and special precautions must be taken. Covers for hay holes, guards on machinery, and keeping certain areas off limits for little children are just a few necessary precautions. Every year more reports surface of accidents on farms and shops where children are hurt or killed, many of which could have been avoided.

As Dan drove out to the orchard with the skid loader, his mind was on the tasks ahead of him. He was not thinking about his children as they had stayed in the house with Mom that morning. As he neared the trash pile at the far end of the orchard, he was distracted by a rabbit that suddenly jumped out of the grass on his left and hopped a few paces, then sat still and watched him pass. Coming back to the present, he noticed that he had missed the turn. Without hesitation, he pulled the levers back and started backing up to where he had missed the rutted path. But something didn't feel right. He stopped, climbed out of the skid loader and walked around to see if there was anything behind him. His heart jumped into his throat when he saw his two little boys holding a lunch pail directly behind the skid loader, innocently laughing at his shock when he saw them. The boys were surprised at the show of emotion when Daddy suddenly got down on the ground with them and held them tightly for a few moments.

Dan was a sober man as he took the boys back into the house to Mom. God had protected his family. How easily it could have been different. He realized how important it was to let his wife know what he was doing, so that she would not send the boys out when he was operating dangerous machinery.

Unfortunately, there have been cases where the ending was not as pleasant as Dan's story. We believe that God is always in control, and we may not understand why He sometimes allows accidents to happen. However, we have a duty to make sure we do our best in keeping our family safe.

Occasionally the officials charge the parents with "abuse by neglect" when it appears an accident could have been avoided by using proper precautions. Being aware of and following these precautions and safety rules is the least we can do for our children.

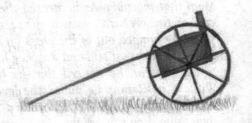

Our close community structure

We would likely all agree that one of the greatest strengths of our Plain communities is our close community structure and culture. We do not live to ourselves, but are part of a sheltering and loving community where each of us has our place and we are, for the most part, comfortable within that culture. This is one of the reasons we have been able to withstand many of the negative outside influences of the world. Having a distinct culture apart from the popular culture of the world around us reduces the pressures and influences we would otherwise be subjected to.

But for those caught in abusive situations, this can actually make it much harder. They may feel trapped in a situation where no one hears them. Everyone else has their place within that culture, and they have seemingly slipped through the cracks. You may have heard the saying, "The loneliest place in the world is in the middle of a crowd where everyone else belongs and you are left out."

> *The Millers had a string of daughters. They were finally blessed with a son, and as he grew, he proved to be very responsible and capable. Even at a young age, his parents*

were able to give him responsibilities around the house. There was no doubt about it, he was the apple of his father's eye. Even the neighbors commented on how proud the father must be of such a son. The son thrived on this attention. Sometimes he took his privilege too far and was physically abusive toward others when no one was looking.

A few years later, the Millers were blessed with another son. This son was the exact opposite of his older brother. With his happy-go-lucky nature, he didn't seem to take anything seriously. It seemed he was always getting into some kind of trouble and doing things for attention. At the age when his brother would have been sent down the road with the pony and pony cart, the younger brother was not allowed to drive the pony even if an adult was along because "he wasn't fit." Needless to say, the more his father let the younger brother know that he wished he were more like his older brother, the more inferior he felt, and the less he acted responsible like his older brother. He resorted to unorthodox ways of seeking attention, such as telling stories that were not quite true.

Occasionally, his older brother would become particularly exasperated with him and beat him up. One time, the younger son complained to his parents and his parents called in his older brother for his side of the story. The older son denied hurting his younger brother and said, in fact, his younger brother had hit him first. It soon became obvious that somebody was not telling the truth. Since the parents were used to believing their older son, the younger son was punished for lying.

As you can imagine, a cycle of vying for attention, of abuse, and then of feeling that no one cares anyway, took its toll on the second son. In a society that prided itself on its strong community spirit, one of their own was trapped by that same community spirit. Praise the Lord, in this case, a caring person noticed what was happening and took the younger son under his wings in time to direct him onto a better path.

Romans 15:1 says, "We then that are strong ought to bear the infirmities of the weak..." By the grace of God, may we who are strong be as this caring person. May God raise up more who are willing to notice and reach out in love.

The headship order within the church and home

Another strength for us as Plain people is the Biblical application of the headship order within the church. From passages like Ephesians 5 and 1 Corinthians 11, we can outline the order in this way: *God – Christ – Husband – Wife – Children*. It is one of the bedrocks upon which our culture has been built. As long as this order is properly and lovingly maintained, there is no better way.

However, just like any other Biblical concept, this principle can be abused. Two thousand years ago, Peter said of the writings of Paul, "Which they that are unlearned and unstable wrest, as they do also the other scriptures, unto their own destruction."[4]

Ever since the time of Constantine, the history of the church is littered with examples of those who have abused their power under the guise of following this headship order. Throughout history, there have been churches, leaders, and husbands and wives who have misused and perverted this commandment of God.

Bishop Aaron sat at the kitchen table with bowed head as the early evening sunshine created shadows across the floor. His thoughts rehashed the evening that had just passed. A man and wife from his district had just left after another counseling session. It seemed Aaron just couldn't get through to the young couple. The husband blamed his wife for disobeying him as the head of the household, while the wife blamed him for being unreasonable and harsh. As Aaron mused over some of the things they had said about each other, he couldn't help but recognize how childish they were in their complaints. It was like two children with each trying to be on top. As they had read through Ephesians 5, he had tried to help them realize that mutual love and respect are more important than who had the final say when decisions needed to be made. It seemed he could not get this young couple to realize that a marriage was not a one-way street.

Just then, a little boy poked his head in the door. Seeing his Dad at the table, he yelled, "Hey Dad, there's a balloon coming down in the neighbor's hayfield, and me and Edna wants to go and watch!" Excitedly he tramped over to his dad, forgetting his muddy boots. A trail of mud splotched up the kitchen floor as he went. Aaron looked up in time to see his wife come in the other door, and he noticed the

---

4 2 Peter 3:16

dismayed look on her face.

Without a second thought Aaron thundered, "AARON RAY JUNIOR, look at the kitchen floor that Mom just cleaned! Now get out of here with your muddy boots, and you are not going anywhere since you aren't responsible enough to take off your boots when you come in the house." Junior turned his face up toward his dad in shock, took one look at his angry face, and made a quick retreat back out the door, spreading more mud as he nearly stumbled over his own boots in his haste.

There was a moment of silence, then his wife spoke, almost bossily, it seemed to Aaron. "I think you need to go out and comfort your little boy. Weren't you a little harsh with him?"

Aaron looked at his wife in surprise. Here he was trying to get his youngest son to respect his wife's kitchen, and she didn't even appreciate it! Again he responded without a second thought. "Okay, if that's how you feel, I guess I'll just let them traipse mud over everything from now on."

Wisely, his wife didn't respond. Aaron got up and left for the barn. A man can't even be the boss in his own house anymore, he thought to himself. After all, who's the boss around here? Just then he thought he heard a sob. Carefully, he stepped closer to the washhouse door and peeked in. There was his son, sobbing as he tried to pull his boots off. Aaron's heart smote him, and suddenly he realized that his wife had been right. He had been too harsh. After all, how often did a hot air balloon land in the neighbor's hay field? Small wonder that Junior had forgotten about his muddy boots. Was it just tonight that he had explained to the young husband and wife that the proper headship order does not mean that one can harshly rule over his family? That just as Jesus is the head of the church with love unbounded, so should a husband's love be toward his wife and children? It all starts and ends with love.

With a determined look on his face, he stepped into the washhouse and strode over toward his son. Junior looked up with fearful eyes, then surprise registered on his face as his dad said to him, "Here, leave your boots on, you'll need them to go along over to the hayfield to watch that balloon."

The smile that came through the tears was all the reward that Aaron needed. As he knelt down to help pull the boot back on, he said gruffly, "I'm sorry I yelled at you. It's easy to forget when something as exciting as a balloon comes around, isn't it?"

Aaron's heart was filled with gratitude as they headed over the field toward the large balloon. How ready little children were to forgive and forget. Junior chattered excitedly as they hurried through the wet hayfield. How blessed he was. Somehow he knew that his wife would be just as ready to forgive when he apologized to her later.

How easy it is for us to use our position of authority in a way that hurts others rather than helps them. We need to have the same love for our families that Jesus has for the church, and if we fail sometimes, we need to be willing to make things right as Aaron was in the example above.

To put this in the proper perspective, we need to ask ourselves: Does the fact that the headship order has often been abused prove that this order is wrong? Is not the abuse of power the real problem?

Proper child discipline

A real strength in maintaining our community respect and culture over the years has been using child discipline. A child who knows where his boundaries are, and that he needs to respect

> Just as a shepherd uses his rod in many ways as he herds his sheep; likewise, there are many ways that a child may be disciplined.

those boundaries, is usually a happier and more contented child than one who often ends up getting his own way. Solomon tells us in Proverbs 13:24, "He that spareth his rod hateth his son: but he that loveth him chasteneth him betimes." Just as a shepherd uses his rod in many ways as he herds his sheep; likewise, there are many ways that a child may be disciplined. But one thing is clear from this proverb: if a parent truly loves his child, he will not withhold discipline when it becomes necessary. Proverbs also says, "The rod and reproof give wisdom: but a child left to himself bringeth his mother to shame."[5]

But just as it is possible to misuse the headship order, so it is possible to misuse child discipline. Punishing a child when we are upset is counterproductive. It is a truth that has been passed to us by our forefathers down through the generations: "*Wait to punish a child until you are no longer upset.*"

A writer in our local newspaper, trying to impress upon her readers that it would be improper to physically punish a child, told of the incident that caused her to abandon paddling as a means of punishing her own child. "I happened to catch a glimpse," she wrote, "of my face in the mirror while I was paddling my child. I decided then and there that I would never stoop so low again."[6]

---

[5] Proverbs 29:15
[6] The author remembers a letter to the editor in the *Lancaster Intelligencer Journal* in the early 2000's.

Most of us would agree that this writer's real problem was her anger. We would maintain that punishing her child in anger was abuse, whatever mode of punishment she was using.

Too often, when a parent punishes in anger, the message they are inadvertently conveying is that it is okay for a larger person to hurt a smaller one.

Punishing in anger gives the child the wrong message. Furthermore, when we punish in anger, we often do not have control of our emotions and actions as we should and we cause more hurt to the child than we ever intended (for more on this, see the chapter on "Positive Parenting.")

Chapter 2

Types of Child Abuse & Neglect

John's mind was reeling as he headed down the road to the bank. The news had just reached him that Sam, a trusted middle-aged neighbor, had been arrested for child abuse. How could Sam, good old Sam, who appeared to be an upstanding member of the community and the church, be guilty of such a crime?

As John mulled over the news that he had just heard, he thought back over the years during which their children had gone to school together. Sam's children were frequently involved in troublemaking at school and John was always puzzled by this. They seemed to need so much more attention than the other children. "Almost," thought John, "as if they were crying out for love. Or were they crying out for help? And no one understood!" John shook his head in confusion. Why had no one understood? "All we saw," he mused, "was a child that needed a good spanking so they would snap out of it. We had no idea."

As John drove past a large Mennonite elementary school, the playground was swarming with children. The air was filled with the sound of laughter and shouting, and suddenly punctuated by the shrill sound of a teacher's whistle. John supposed that there were over a hundred children going to this school. A little farther down the road he passed another school, a small parochial school with perhaps 30 or so pupils. Through the window he could see a few of the pupils at their desks. He knew most of these children and their parents, as this was the school where his own children had attended. There was a second room in this school that served as a "special ed" school for the community. John could not help thinking over the words that his neighbor had spoken when he had told him about Sam's arrest.

"Well, John," he had said with a hint of a smirk on his face, "You Mennonites and Amish aren't so different from the rest of us after all. I read in the newspaper that in America today, 1 in 4 girls, 1 in 7 boys, and 1 in 2 mentally handicapped children will be abused by the age of 18. And I don't expect that youn's are any different."

John surely hoped he was wrong. As he tried to grasp what these numbers meant, he thought of the schools he had just passed. If these figures were true, at least 30 of those carefree children would end up as victims of abuse.

Defining abuse and neglect

Abuse is when someone intentionally harms a child; neglect is when a child is harmed because someone failed to protect or provide for them.

We may think of an abuser as a stranger on the street, but most abuse happens by someone the child knows. Often the abuser is a family member, a neighbor, or a relative. And quite often, the child will not tell anyone. In a later chapter, we will discuss some of the reasons for this.

Child abuse is defined in the United States as, "Any recent act or failure to act on the part of a parent or caretaker which results in death, serious physical or emotional harm, sexual abuse or exploitation or an act or failure to act

Four types of abuse:
1. Neglect
2. Emotional abuse
3. Physical abuse
4. Sexual abuse

which presents an imminent risk of serious harm." A "child" generally means a person who is younger than age 18, and an "adult" generally means a person who is 18 or older.[7]

There are four types of abuse which have been researched and recognized.

Neglect

Neglect is when a child gets hurt because of something his parents or caretakers didn't do. They did not supervise him closely enough, give him proper medical attention, or provide for his daily needs. Perhaps they failed to provide a safe place for the child.

In the world today, more children die of neglect than any other type of abuse. Now we would expect this to be less common in our Plain communities because of our close community and family structures. However, neglect can be more than a child starving because of a parent's inability to feed him. Consider the following:

Failure to provide a safe environment for our children to work and play. Every year, children in our communities are seriously hurt or killed in farm or shop accidents. Increasingly, Social

Child Welfare Information Gateway

Services is questioning whether appropriate safeguards are being utilized to prevent these accidents.

Because the practice of having our children work with their parents as they grow up is such an integral part of the Old Order culture, it can be hard to know when children should be allowed to accompany adults during daily chores and duties. We need to realize, however, that farming and some other occupations are more dangerous now than they were in the past. When trying to decide whether children should be present for a particular job, we should consider all the safety factors. There are machines we use in our homes and businesses today that require extra precautions. For those of us who farm with horses, have we taught our children proper respect for such a large animal? Do we have the habit of checking that there are no children around when we use large machinery?

There are many ways we can make our farms and places of business safer, such as having proper hayhole covers, fences around manure pits, shields on machinery, locked doors, etc.

There was a time when we could send our very young children to the neighbors without fear of them getting hit on the roads. But this is no longer advisable in most of our communities. For many of us it may be necessary to have some kind of fence along the road if we have young children. Many communities are encouraging school children to wear reflective vests when walking to and from school. We do well to make sure the younger children always have someone older to walk with. In some cases, it may be necessary to maintain special lanes so children do not need to walk so close to traffic along a busy highway.

It is easy to take for granted that children know the traffic and safety rules when they start driving or riding a pony. But on today's busy roads, we need to make sure our children are mature enough to handle situations that may come up. It is important that we do so before allowing them to drive even on a lonely country road, and much more so on a busy road. Teaching our children the "rules of the road" is time well spent.

In recent years, authorities have been on the alert for accidents that occurred because of underage children who were left unattended. We may think our children are responsible enough to take care of themselves while we run to the neighbors. However, there is a real danger in leaving our younger children in the care of their siblings who are still young children themselves. Not all children mature at the same rate, but with the public eye on us as never before, leaving preschool children in the care of a 10-year-old would certainly not be advisable.

Refusing to take proper medical action. This is another area where we need to be careful. Many of us are not eager to take our children to a medical doctor for every little thing. Rather, we prefer to first try traditional home remedies and other natural methods of treatments. In many cases, there is nothing wrong with this approach. However, there have been cases where Social Services has charged parents with abuse by neglect when it appeared that parents *refused to take proper medical action* that may have prevented a serious illness or death of a child. Remember, sometimes medical intervention is necessary, not only to satisfy the Social Services, but for the well-being of our children.

Allowing our children too much time together without adult supervision. Periodically checking up on our children when they are playing in the barn by themselves, or when groups of them are together at an auction or on a Sunday afternoon, is not being nosy. It is being a concerned parent. There have been many cases of abuse over the years when groups of children have had too much idle time or when we have left our young children to be supervised by their older siblings when the older ones were not as mature as we gave them credit for.

<u>Failing to take time to train and teach our children.</u> Last but not least, this is the worst form of abuse by neglect for those of us within the Old Order culture. The best way to train them is by having them with us. They learn their most important lessons by observing our attitudes, actions, and reactions in all our everyday situations. There are also times when we need to teach them by talking with them, and warning them of the dangers that they will meet, both physically and spiritually.

Emotional Abuse

Emotional abuse happens when a child is hurt emotionally by our actions and words.

We learn most of our parenting skills from our parents, from the way that we ourselves were raised. As stated earlier, in most cases this is the best way. But what if you grew up in a dysfunctional home, where a father or mother controlled their children by making them feel guilty or inferior, and by constantly putting them down? How do you suppose such a child will raise their own children years down the road? It is a cycle that could continue generation after generation. Such children often grow up with an inferior sense of self-worth (a proper feeling of self-worth is not the same as pride).

Emotional abuse causes a child to feel inadequate, powerless, and inferior, and they will often react in wrong ways to situations that other children would accept as a matter of fact. Often such children will have difficulty trusting and forming healthy relationships with others. It is not unusual for them to in turn abuse others or to emotionally withdraw.

Emotional abuse can be hard to define, but here are a few things that we could define as emotional abuse:

- Punishing in anger

- Yelling at our children
- Unusual or harsh punishments that do not fit the crime
- Talking degradingly about our children in front of others (or at any time, as far as that goes)
- Any action or conversation that makes our children feel inferior
- Bullying and teasing

Emotional abuse is generally a factor in almost all the other kinds of abuse as well.

Physical Abuse

Physical abuse happens when a child is hurt by someone older, bigger, or stronger than themselves, especially if it causes an injury such as a broken bone, burn, or bruise. Our children, especially our younger ones, will often get scrapes and bruises from everyday activities. When marks appear on the knees, elbows, or foreheads, we may need to care for them, but we do not typically need to worry that they were caused by abuse. However, when the marks are on the cheeks, chest, back, or buttocks, we may rightly suspect abuse. We should be especially alarmed when the marks don't match the description given for how they appeared.

Physical abuse may result in injuries that require medical attention and may even leave scars. A child who is being physically abused often has an undue fear of the person who is abusing them. As in emotional abuse, such a child may in turn hurt or bully others, or may withdraw.

Physical discipline may not cause marks or physically harm the child in any way.

In the U.S. and Canada, it is still permissible to use physical punishment (paddling) to discipline our children. However, such punishments are not allowed to leave marks or to physically harm the child in any way. And, in most states and provinces, any punishment that causes undue pain is prohibited.

Most of us understand that raising godly children is so much more than merely punishing wrongdoing. Physical abuse can happen so easily when a parent knows no other way of responding to their misbehaving child other than spanking. As we will discuss more fully in a later chapter, a child should feel secure in his parent's love. Any punishment should be a reinforcement of that love, whether the punishment is physical or some other form of punishment. It should never make the child fearful of the parent. Any punishment administered simply to appease the anger of the parent can and should be viewed as abuse.

If paddling is to be used at all, it should be the punishment of last resort, only one of many tools in the toolbox of child training.

Sexual Abuse

To explain what sexual abuse is, let us quote from a typical state manual[8]:

> *The law says: Intentionally, knowingly or recklessly causing sexual abuse or exploitation of a child through any act or failure to act. What this means: Causing a child to engage in or to assist another individual to engage in sexually explicit conduct as well as conversation. The sex acts don't actually have to occur. Activities such as talking about, pretending, demonstrating, depicting, or modeling would all be considered sex acts. The law also says that creating the likelihood of sexual abuse through any recent act or failure to act is considered child abuse.*

Why should it be necessary to talk about sexual abuse in a book for the Old Order Amish and Mennonites? According to the

---

[8] Pennsylvania Child Abuse Training Manual, 2015

24

records of the CCI,[9] over 50% of abuse cases reported among the Amish and Mennonites and other conservative Anabaptist groups in Pennsylvania is for sexual abuse.

A recent case that hit the headlines was of two Amish girls in the state of New York who were abducted and sexually abused. A wave of fear swept through many communities, and parents were freshly reminded to warn their children never to go with strangers. However, the sad truth is, only a very small percentage of abuse cases are by strangers.[10] Most sexual abuse is perpetrated by parents, relatives, or close friends of the child.

How can this be possible?

We live in a fallen world. We have a God who is holy and pure. He has created all things to be holy and pure. However, we have an enemy who has been rejected by God, and who would do anything within his power to hinder God's kingdom. Is it any wonder this enemy would try to take anything that God has created as holy and pure, and try to make it unholy, defiled, and dirty?

The more pure and holy something is, the more Satan would have it defiled and dirty. That is what he is doing if he manages to get us to use God's holy name in vain, use dirty language, or give in to any twisted desires.

Let us allow our minds to roam for a bit. Can we, in our mind's eye, see a cluster of men or boys standing outside a horse barn? Suddenly there is an outburst of raucous laughter. Is there any chance that just now Satan has managed to make a sacred subject dirty?

And are we then surprised when abuse happens among us?

Ephesians 5 has much to say about foolish talking, filthiness, and how it is a shame even to speak of illicit things. Paul wrote

---

[9] Conservative Crisis Intervention: An organization appointed by the Old Order Amish and Mennonite churches in Pennsylvania to work with abuse cases within their churches.

[10] U.S. Department of Health and Human Services, Administration on Children, Youth and Families, *Child Maltreatment 2008* (Washington DC: U.S. Government Printing Office, 2010)

this 2,000 years ago, but it is as true today as it was then. How many young people have struggled with impure thoughts and were on the brink of victory? Then, because they heard adults – professing Christians – make light of this sacred subject, they needed to start the battle all over again.

How is it possible that this has become such a scourge in many of our Plain communities? "Be not deceived, God is not mocked, for whatsoever a man soweth, that shall he also reap" (Galatians 6:7). Inappropriate jokes and dirty talk lead to inappropriate thoughts. Inappropriate thoughts lead to impure desires. Impure desires will have an effect on the individual. "Can a man take fire in his bosom, and his clothes not be burned?" (Proverbs 6:27). Is it too hard to understand that impure desires can eventually lead to inappropriate actions?

Like other types of abuse, sexual abuse has devastating effects for the child. So often the child will keep the abuse secret, often for many years, and sometimes they never tell.

Many of those who have been abused are able to cover it up at the time. They hide it and try not to think about it. It is just too terrible to think about, so they pretend it never happened and block it from their minds. There have actually been cases where they have been so successful in this that they have difficulty in later years remembering any of the details. However, it is not possible to erase the emotional scars. Many times, years later, when other pressures of life become overwhelming, the effects and memories of the abuse suddenly come back full force. For women, this sometimes happens once they are married and experience the normal pressures of raising a family.

> To a child, in many cases sexual abuse has more to do with broken trust than it does physical actions.

Even though we may think of abusers as being male and the abused as being female, this is not always the case. Many boys have been sexually abused over the years, and it is just as damaging to a male as it is for a female. Also, there are cases of girls or women as abusers.

To a child, in many cases the abuse has much more to do with broken trust than it does physical actions. An abused child may have a hard time building relationships, often for the rest of their lives. Even in marriage, they may find it hard to really trust and love their marriage partner, because the sacredness of the marriage bond has been defiled, and the memory of being taken advantage of is so real to them.

An abused child will often react differently to situations that other children can shrug off. Innocent little things can trigger a host of poorly buried emotions and feelings. Their conscience has been seared, and the concepts of a loving God, and of forgiveness, trust, and close friendships, are almost impossible for them to grasp.

The damage that is done in a few minutes of gratification by a person with impure desires is hard to describe. However, God is not mocked; what a man sows that shall he also reap.[11]

But why must so much of the reaping be done by the abused rather than the abuser?

---

[11] Galatians 6:7

Chapter 3

Recognizing Abuse

Ruth remembers the uneasy feelings she had whenever Elwood was around her children. Elwood had moved into the community a few years earlier. He was a pleasant, middle-aged man with a big smile. Ruth had noticed soon after he moved into the area that he had a special attraction to small children. He always seemed to have candy along, and would give the children lots of attention. What made Ruth uncomfortable was the way he would pull children unto his lap and whisper to them, trying to gain their confidence. Once on a Sunday afternoon, she had heard him suggest to a little girl that they could go for a walk through the woods. She couldn't put her finger on it, but she knew that something just didn't seem quite right. Even though she never mentioned anything to other adults, she warned her own children to stay away from him, and whenever he was around, she kept a close eye on them.

It was not until almost a year later that she learned that her premonitions were correct. Elwood was no longer allowed to

> be at home with his family because of his actions, which the
> officials described as "corruption of minors."

> How thankful Ruth was that she had followed her intuition
> and kept her children safe. On the other hand, she felt a
> twinge of guilt. Should she have spoken up when she noticed
> that something wasn't quite right? Would that have spared
> someone else's child?

Recognizing abuse is not always easy. And the last thing we
want is to be suspicious of everyone we meet. However, there are
signs that we should be aware of. In this chapter, we would like to
uncover some of these signs.

We do need to remember that many of the signs and symptoms
an abused child will exhibit are similar to behaviors that children
exhibit as they go through normal stages of development. Also
some children will not exhibit these signs, even though they are
being abused.

Often abuse is not something that happens at random. Most
children who experience abuse experience it over an extended
period of time. Abusers will often "groom" their intended victim,
perhaps over a period of weeks or months, or sometimes even for
years. They may do this by gradually moving from appropriate to
inappropriate conduct. The relationship may seem entirely
appropriate at first. Compliments. Making the child feel important.
Giving them candy or gifts. This is often followed by gradually
drawing them in. Holding their hand. Touching them in
increasingly inappropriate ways. Abusers are often great
manipulators. The child is not fully aware of how things have
progressed to where they are and doesn't know how to put a stop
to it.

Now wouldn't it seem that a child would be quick to tell
someone if they were being abused? Certainly he would not clam
up and keep the abuse a secret?

The sad fact is, this is exactly what often happens. Most of the time, an abused child will never tell anyone, and if they are asked about it, they will staunchly deny it. Why?

There are several reasons.

1. It is not unusual for the child to feel at least partly responsible. Therefore, even though it's not true, they feel guilty, as if it were partly their own fault. So.... it becomes a dirty little secret they dare not talk about, and the longer it goes, the harder it becomes.

2. Another reason may be because the abuser is someone they like, someone who makes them feel loved and accepted when no one else seems to care. They might not like the abuse, but wish to avoid getting their "friend" into trouble.

3. Sometimes, it is because of fear. They actually fear the abuser and the power he or she has over them. If it is a parent or another authority figure, they may fear what will happen if they tell. If it is a brother or sister, uncle, neighbor, or some other friend of the family, he may have threatened them with consequences if they tell. The child may also fear what will happen to their family's reputation.

4. Depending on the type of abuse, a child may not know they are being abused. A young child's whole world is wrapped up in his own experiences and his own family, so he may not realize that other children are not experiencing the same things he is experiencing. This is especially true in a family where physical and emotional abuse are present.

Even though it is rare that a child will come right out and tell others about the abuse in a way that we understand, she may be crying out for help in ways that we may not hear. All we see is a naughty, sullen, rebellious, withdrawn, or snooty child. We see a child who needs a good spanking to help them "snap out of it." As we become more aware of the symptoms of abuse, we will perhaps be better able to hear their underlying cry for help.

In summary, let us list some of the signs of abuse that we should learn to recognize—

Signs of abuse:
1. Sudden changes in the child's behavior or personality.
2. A child suddenly does not want to go certain places.
3. Child develops an unnatural interest in sexuality.
4. Unusual or unexplained bruises on a child.

Rule #1: <u>Be aware of sudden changes in behavior or personality, especially if a child becomes overly aggressive or passive</u>.

Sometimes the child becomes withdrawn or moody. Their grades in school may plummet. Or perhaps they will get into all kinds of trouble, almost as if they are wanting to get caught.

Be aware if a child becomes overly aggressive or passive. Some children are by nature more aggressive than others. But if a child becomes overly aggressive, displaying abusive behavior or speech to other people or even animals, there may be an underlying reason. On the other hand, it is just as much a warning sign if a child suddenly becomes overly passive or withdrawn, exhibiting either a fearful or an "I don't care" attitude.

Rule #2: <u>Be aware if a child suddenly does not want to go certain places.</u>

Be aware if a child suddenly does not want to go certain places, such as to a particular neighbor, to Grandpa's place, or home. Here again, it is not unusual for children to go through phases where they would rather not go to certain places, but we dare not ignore it if this happens. Remember, an abused child, if asked directly, will almost always deny the abuse. It takes great wisdom, tact, and patience to get a child to talk about what makes them fearful.

Rule #3: <u>Be aware if a child develops an unnatural interest in sexuality.</u>

Be aware if a child suddenly develops an unnatural interest in sexuality. There are stages in a child's development where a moderate curiosity about sexuality is normal, and parents need to respond in a healthy way to questions. However, if a child engages in inappropriate sexual play, drawings, or other actions that are unusual for their age or development, there may very well be an underlying reason that should be investigated.

Rule #4: <u>Be aware of unusual or unexplained bruises on a child</u>.

Be aware of unusual or unexplained bruises on a child. We do not want to become suspicious of every bruise a child receives. Some children are more prone to accidents than others, and some overly active children seem to frequently show up with cuts and bruises somewhere or the other. However, it may be an indicator of abuse if a pattern of bruises or other injuries develops in a child (particularly if the bruises have unbelievable or inconsistent explanations; or, the bruises appear on areas of the body where they should not normally happen).

Again, we would like to say that many of the signs and

symptoms of abuse we have discussed may be similar to behaviors children exhibit as they go through the normal stages of childhood development. Also, sometimes these signs and behaviors will not be present even though the child has been or is being abused. Just because a child exhibits one or more of the symptoms we have discussed in this chapter does not automatically mean they are being abused. We do not want to go to the other extreme and be suspicious of every person or situation we meet.

So how can we know? When should we take action? When should we ignore the unusual behaviors, and when should we become concerned?

We would like to suggest that it would be better to err on the side of protecting our children. We should never ignore unusual behaviors. This does not mean that we need to overreact every time we see one of these behaviors, but it does mean we will lovingly probe and talk with our children when such signs appear. We should be aware of these signs if we are teachers or are engaged in regularly scheduled activities with children in some other way.

What if we feel that something is not right within a family but there is no conclusive evidence? Can we do something for a child in this situation?

Ideally, we would desire for every child to have a "trusted" adult to go to. The most trusted adults in a child's life should be his or her parents. In an ideal setting, there is an additional network of trusted adults in a child's life. Church, community, extended family, and friends are all a part of the trusted network that surrounds most children in our Plain communities. But what about a child who has fallen through the cracks, where, perhaps the parents are part of the problem? What if the child has been taught it is not safe to go to anyone else? Is there a way we could reach out to such a child without completely alienating the family?

We are not speaking of obvious abuse that needs to be reported, but of an emotionally needy child who may be crying out for the love and acceptance that is somehow missing in his or her life. We may know the family situation is not ideal, and that probing too much may cause the family to withdraw and thus isolate the child even more. Is there a way we can reach out in such a situation?

Again, all children need a trusted adult in their lives. We may feel there is nothing we can do. Let us remind you of what Mordecai said to Esther, "And who knoweth whether thou art come to the kingdom for such a time as this?"[12]

Teachers, concerned neighbors, unmarried aunts, cousins, or whoever you may be, are you the person God has chosen to make a difference in a child's life? What this child may need is simply an understanding person. Do not probe too deeply into his life. Just be there. Become the "trusted friend" that he may eventually feel comfortable coming to if things become unbearable or something more serious happens in his life.

In a later chapter, we will discuss the committees that have been organized in some of our communities to deal with abuse. These committees should be made up of safe people to go to if we have questions, concerns, or if we simply need to discuss a situation. They can also help us report to the proper authorities.

---

[12] Esther 4:14

Chapter 4

Positive Parenting

Ben would never forget the time his two oldest children avoided a serious disaster because of their unquestioning prompt obedience. He had been driving a young horse that still needed more training, something which he greatly enjoyed. This particular horse had developed a fear of trucks, but Ben had always been able to keep him under control. The horse was doing fine lately, so when his children came running for a ride, he decided to take them along. He waited till they had climbed on to the front seat beside him on the open spring wagon.

As they headed out on the road, three trucks came roaring past. The young horse reared and tried to go off to the side, but with careful maneuvering, Ben kept him on the road. Just after this, an especially noisy truck came up from behind and started passing. This time, the horse lost his head, and instead of veering off to the side, he tried to take off in a dead gallop to get away from the terrible monster that was passing him. Ben held on to the lines with a firm hand and spoke softly to the horse to calm him. And then suddenly, to his horror, he felt the left line give way. Ben took in the situation in an instant. On the right side of the road was a steep bank that dropped down a good ten feet. If he pulled on the remaining right line, he would surely guide the horse down that bank with disastrous results.

The horse, feeling that he was suddenly free, completely lost his head now and, after a barely perceptible pause, decided to take off. This was a busy road, and unless Ben managed to somehow regain control of the horse, a disaster was likely to happen. So in that moment before the horse took off at a dead gallop, he turned to his two children beside him, who at this point did not yet realize that anything was going on. He spoke quietly but forcefully, "Jump off the wagon, RIGHT NOW!"

Ben's two children paused only a moment before scrambling to the side and back and took a flying leap off the spring wagon. The oldest one jumped off the side and tumbled down the steep embankment, rolling over and over before coming to a stop at the bottom, then jumping up to see what the excitement was all about. The second one jumped off the back, and because of the speed they were going was thrown off balance. She bumped her head on the road, but then scrambled up to join her sister in watching the horse and wagon.

The horse, in the meantime, took off at top speed. Ben also jumped, but before he let go of the lines, he accidentally jerked on them and guided the horse toward the side of the road. At the next electric pole, the horse himself narrowly missed the pole. The spring wagon did not miss, however, but crashed full speed into the pole at the very spot where Ben's two girls had been sitting just seconds before.

In the end, nothing much more serious happened. The horse

> *was headed off by some neighbor boys and was caught in the next barnyard. Of course, the spring wagon required extensive repairs, but no one was seriously hurt beyond a few scrapes and bruises from jumping off at such a high speed.*

> *Ben knew that not all children would respond with such unquestioning obedience, and he felt very fortunate they had responded so quickly.*

The point here is that there was one overwhelming reason that Ben's children obeyed in time to avoid a possible disaster. And that reason was trust. Certainly the children had been taught obedience, but just as certainly, they trusted their father and did not question his judgment. Remember, at the time when they were asked to jump, they had no idea why. As they later said, they did not realize that anything unusual had happened. Children do not usually respond so quickly because of fear of an overly strict parent. These girls jumped, not only because they were used to obeying their father, but, more importantly because they had learned to trust him. They knew without thinking that if he asked them to jump from a fast-moving wagon "RIGHT NOW," he must have a reason that was beyond dispute.

Actions speak so much louder than words. Because their dad always took time to care for his children before thinking of himself, they knew without thinking about it that they were secure in his care and love.

That is what we would like to stress in this chapter. Having a healthy, loving atmosphere in our home that is built on mutual respect and affection and loving discipline is at the heart of protecting our children from abuse. Many children who are abused come from families where such love is not present or where the parents have not learned how to affirm their love to their children.

Having a healthy, loving atmosphere in the home that is built on mutual respect and affection and loving discipline is at the heart of protecting our children from abuse...The best prevention against abuse is positive parenting.

Remember the grooming that often precedes abusing a child? The truth is, it is hard to "groom" a child who is not "needy," who feels comfortable and secure in her parent's love. The best prevention against abuse is positive parenting.

It is impossible in one short chapter to do justice to the topic of positive parenting. Entire books have been written on Biblical child training, a few of which we recommend (see the appendix at the end of the book).

Most parents love their children dearly. So why is it that some of us in the Plain communities have a hard time expressing this love? It has been said the most important thing a father can do for his children is to love their mother. It is just as important that the mother love the father. A stable home environment makes for well-adapted children who are not emotionally "needy." But for the children to feel comfortable in their parents' love, they need to know they are loved. Learning to express this love to children may come naturally for some parents, while others may need to "learn" how to do it. Also, some children may seem to need more love than others, when really what they need is more reassurance of our love. Let us look at some of the ways to make our children feel secure and loved.

1. **Having time for our children**.

Children feel valued if their parents take time for them. When our children talk, we should give them our full attention. Laying aside that paper, or stopping our work for a few moments to look into our child's eyes and listen to what they have to say, is giving our child the message that they are valued and loved.

2. **Physical touch**.

Hugging or reassuringly holding their hand lets children know we love them. As they grow older, something as simple as a hand on the shoulder at the right moment can speak volumes.

3. **Verbalizing our love**.

Often, reassuring our children that we love them is as simple as saying so out loud. Telling our children we love them should be done often when they are small. As they grow older, there are many other ways of verbalizing our love. Love can also be conveyed through common courtesies, such as saying, "Thank you," "Excuse me," or "That's great!"

It is possible for parents to say "I love you" to their children, but then fail to show it. However, verbalizing our love to our children should always be one the of many expressions of our love.

4. **Including our children**.

By including our children in discussions, decisions, and activities, we are telling them we trust them, and that they are valued as part of the family unit. Of course, they cannot be included in every discussion or decision, but the value of making it a habit to include them where we can should not be underestimated.

5. **Positive reinforcement**.

Encouraging good behavior is often more effective than discouraging wrong behavior. While proper discipline is important, finding ways to encourage our children when they do something right, or when we notice they are trying, can often make other methods of discipline less necessary.

6. **Being consistent**.

Some children seem to need more reinforcement of our love than others. It is important, however, that parents show the same amount of love to all of their children. It is not unusual for one child to be milder and another to get into all kinds of scrapes and mischief. It is easy for parents to show less love to the child who is in trouble all the time. This is exactly the opposite of what that child needs in many cases. The misdemeanors should be properly dealt with, and then put behind us. If a misbehaving child is continuously made to feel guilty or inferior, it is making them ripe for abuse from others.

7. **Using proper discipline**.

The wise man Solomon said, "The rod and reproof give wisdom: but a child left to himself bringeth his mother to shame."[13]

We realize this is a sensitive subject. Yes, we in Plain communities believe the modern idea of raising children with no physical punishment runs counter to the will and Word of God. And yet, the misuse of physical punishment may be the very reason so many people in our modern world are against spanking.

What we would like to emphasize is that venting our feelings upon a child in anger is teaching them that it's okay for a larger person to hurt a smaller person. As was mentioned in an earlier chapter, any punishment administered simply to appease the anger of the parent can and should be viewed as abuse. Examples include: physical punishment, yelling at our children, giving them the silent treatment, or saying demeaning things about them. We have heard parents say that if they do not punish when they are angry, they no longer have the heart to punish. How sad. What is such a parent teaching their child?

---

[13] Proverbs 29:15

Proper discipline should not automatically mean physical punishment. **A parent should have many ways of disciplining a child other than paddling**. None of these ways should be a means of venting our feelings. If a child can feel we are punishing them because we are angry, it is simply giving the child permission to vent his anger on someone else the next time something does not suit him.

A child who is properly disciplined in love will usually display love and respect for his mother or father after the punishment.

Making our children feel secure and loved:
- Having time for our children
- Physical touch
- Verbalizing our love
- Including our children
- Positive reinforcement
- Being consistent
- Using proper discipline

What does "punishing in love" look like?

First of all, a child needs to understand why he is being punished. This may sound quite obvious, but it is easy to assume that a child knows what he is being punished for when he only partly understands it. It is often necessary to explain why we need to punish them for a particular misdeed.

Also, the punishment needs to match the misdeed. If it was a minor offense, a timeout or other minor punishment may be called for. We should reserve more serious punishments for more serious misdeeds. If a time out has not worked and the behavior continues, obviously the punishment was not enough. The old saying is, "The consequences of the misdeed must be greater than the enjoyment of the misdeed." Sometimes a closer look is warranted. What is the child trying to communicate through their behavior? What is it they need? Is there a natural consequence that might help the child learn appropriate behavior? Also, we parents need to know the different personalities of our children. What may seem to be a serious punishment to one child may not bother the next child.

A punishment should erase the guilt. Once a misdeed has been properly addressed and punished, that event should be put behind us, and the air should be cleared. What better way to give evidence of the love and forgiveness of God toward those who come to Him than for parents to demonstrate that forgiveness to their children.

And last but not least, it is important we reaffirm our love for the child after the punishment. For a younger child, this usually means holding them and telling them that we love them. As the child grows older, there may be other appropriate ways to show that we love them unconditionally. For the older child, the best way to reaffirm our love may be to simply put the incident behind us, and be as friendly and smiling as before, making sure we show our love by our actions.

Charles tells about the time his oldest daughter, Lillian, needed a more serious punishment. It had progressed from her not wanting to obey a minor rule that seemed unnecessary to her, to repeated punishments for the infraction. After one punishment, Lillian became very upset and refused to talk or respond respectfully to her father. Charles realized that something must be done. The situation had now changed from punishing Lillian for the original misdemeanor to dealing with open rebellion.

This time, he decided to wait till the next morning so he would have time to pray about it and get his emotions under control. Early the next morning, before the rest of the children were up, he called her into the living room. Charles and his wife took the time to explain why her rebellion was so harmful, both to others and to herself and why the punishment they needed to use this time was necessary, even though it was hard to punish her as they really did love her.

After the punishment, Charles simply laid his hand on her shoulder and said, "We do love you, Lillian, and hope you can do better now."

Later in the day after Lillian came home from school, they were working on a project together as a family. Charles rejoiced to see that Lillian was her happy, bubbling self again for the first time in many days. It was another reminder of how well children respond to loving discipline and forgiveness. This kind of reaction from his daughter could not have happened if he would have lashed out in anger as he had been tempted to do.

Chapter 5

Prevention of Abuse and Neglect

In this chapter we will focus on some guidelines for keeping our children safe.

Elizabeth ran a market just outside of town. While she was grateful that her children could help her, she was worried about their youngest daughter, Sadie, who was three years old and always so friendly to their customers. Elizabeth set a strict rule with Sadie and her older children that they were never to get into a customer's car.

One day, realizing she hadn't seen Sadie for a few minutes, Elizabeth went looking for her. Sure enough, there was Sadie—she had climbed inside someone's car and was playing with a toy with some other children. Elizabeth realized then that Sadie wasn't yet old enough to understand this important family rule, and she would have to make sure Sadie stayed inside the store with her.

Ways to keep children safe from abuse and neglect—
1. Learn about child development.
2. Provide a safe (childproof) place for young children to play.
3. Develop common sense safety rules for our homes, farms, and shops.
4. Be careful about leaving children alone with someone bigger than them.
5. Don't leave children unsupervised for long periods of time.
6. Make it a habit to ask about children's activities.
7. Don't be too proud to ask for help.

Just as Elizabeth learned that her three-year-old needed more supervision than what she had at first realized, it is important that we as parents learn about child development. Since children are not just young adults but are going through different stages of development as they grow, we need to adjust how we parent them and provide safety for them at each stage.

For the youngest children, it is the parents' responsibility to provide a safe environment. Young children are not mature enough to be aware of many dangers. In today's world, it is a good idea to childproof every part of the home where a young child spends his day.

As a child grows older, training and safety should go hand in hand. We still need to make sure they have a safe place to be, but at the same time we need to teach and enforce safety rules. When is it safe to have a child ride with Daddy on the horse cart, forklift, or tractor? Never? If we give them an occasional ride in the skid loader, will they come running for a ride the next time when we are not aware of it? Likely! In most farms and shops, there are areas that need to be strictly "off limits" to children. Is it enough to tell our children it is not safe to go there? If we have small children, we need to do our part to secure those areas.

Having common sense safety rules for our homes, farms, and

shops could make the difference between safety and an accident, between life as normal and life as a crippled child, and perhaps between life and death.

Another way we can help prevent abuse and neglect is to check up on our children. Is it necessary for groups of children to be together unsupervised for long periods of time on Sunday afternoons, at community auctions, or other social occasions? We cannot stress enough the importance of periodically checking up on them, however much we may trust our children. Many a parent has found out too late that their innocent child was exposed to things that were not so "innocent."

We do well to be very cautious about whom we leave our children with. Always discuss what your children did when they come back home or when company leaves. Even if they have been at a safe place, such as at Grandma's or just over to the neighbors, make it a habit. Don't just start this conversation when they have been somewhere questionable, but make it a normal, expected conversation.

This should just be a natural conversation that shows you are interested in them, not an inquisition that makes the child feel that you are suspicious of their activities. Interacting with your children in this way will make it easier to notice sudden warning signs, such as when a child is evasive about certain activities.

Most of us send our children to our own private schools in the neighborhood. What better way for parents and teachers to work together than in the teaching and care of their children? It is much better than sending them to a large public school. But this will require participation. Nothing is more important than staying involved in our children's lives, asking questions about their day, knowing who their best friends are, staying in contact with the teacher to show our support, faithfully attending parent teacher meetings, and so on. Again, all these should be normal, friendly interactions—simply a way for us to take an interest in our children's lives. If the teacher, board members, and especially our children can feel our openness and concern, they will be much more likely to come to us if situations arise that we should know about.

There may be times when we ourselves are struggling with issues in our lives.

Do not be too proud to ask for help if you as a parent are faced with a situation that seems to be out of your control. Do you feel depressed all the time? Are you emotionally overtaxed? Do you have trouble sleeping at night? Do you have fits of anger that seem to get out of control? Do you have a marriage partner who is having these problems? Do you feel alone with no one who will listen to you? There is help available. You do not need to face these situations alone. Find help. Often the ministry will be only too glad to give support and to guide you to the proper help, if you are brave enough to ask. The home ministry should be our first resource if we face these problems and situations. In addition, there are committees that have been appointed in many of the larger Amish and Mennonite communities that have gained experience and can guide you in the right direction if you need professional help (see Chapter 6).

In earlier chapters, we talked about the positive role models children need as they grow up. And indeed, the most positive way to prevent abuse is to create a safe, loving environment for our family at home. Nothing else can take the place of this. Now let us suggest some specific things we should be teaching our children as they grow.

First, we will mention some of the more general things we need to teach our children.

• We need to teach our children that God loves them and wants them to be safe. God doesn't want bad things to happen to them. God gave them legs to help them run away from trouble or to run toward another child who needs help. God gave them hands to hold a baby when Mama is making supper. God gave them eyes to watch for cars when crossing the street.

• We need to teach them that each child has unique abilities and gifts that are special. They need to be taught to respect themselves and others.

• We need to teach our children words to express their feelings and words to ask for help. And then we need to remember to listen to them. If they don't want to go to someone's house or spend time with someone, ask them why and listen to their answer.

• We need to teach our children that God created them with beautiful bodies. Certain parts of their bodies need to be kept private, but not because those parts are bad or ugly. Being comfortable with the bodies God gave them is an important part of growing up.

There are also some specific things that we should be teaching our children, as the following story illustrates.

Sarah tossed fitfully as she heard the kitchen clock strike the hour in the room below her. Her thoughts went around in a familiar circle, as they had so often in the last weeks. And again her chest felt as though a band were encircling it, and she found it hard to breathe. In her mind's eye, she saw herself facing her cousin as she had on that fateful day several weeks ago. This time, she would not let anything happen. This time, instead of going along with his playful antics, she would stand her ground and firmly tell Dave, "If you touch me again, I am going to scream!" And then she imagined herself scrambling to her feet and heading to the safety of the adults. This time, she marched right over to her mother to tell her of what Dave had tried to do to her.

At this point, her fantasies fell apart, as they always did. The pain in her chest came back full force, and it was hard to breathe as the reality of that day came back to her. She knew she would never have had the courage to tell her mother or anyone else what had happened.

Oh, if only someone would have warned her! Why had her mother, her dear mother who had taught her so many things over the years, not warned her of these kinds of actions? But because this one subject had never been talked about, she had no idea how to respond when Dave had suggested some playful things they could do together. At first it had all seemed okay. Even when he had suggested they go up to the haymow by themselves, she simply had no idea why it would not be okay. After all, Dave was so much older than she, and he had always been so nice to her. She had simply reveled in his attention. She had no reason not to trust him. So when he had suggested some things they could do that didn't seem quite right to her, well, she had no reason not to keep on trusting him.

But now her body had been violated. She instinctively knew that she would never again view her own body in the same way as she had before. Her innocent carefree childhood had been snatched from her in those moments with a cousin whom she had always trusted. Oh why, oh why, had no one ever told her what was okay to touch and what was not? Why had no one ever warned her there were certain things you should never allow others to do to you? What was so terrible about this one subject that no one would ever talk about it unless they wanted to take advantage of you?

How Sarah longed to go to her mother and pour out her

heart as she had so often done in the past when things had bothered her. But this time was different. This was a taboo subject that one simply never talked about. In fact, even if she did gather up the courage to tell her mother, she had no idea how to say it. She had no names for the things that had happened or for the body parts involved. To Sarah, they were shameful, nameless objects that one never mentioned.

Oh, how dirty she felt. And Dave had warned her that because she had done these things with him, she would be in unspeakable trouble if anyone ever found out. The way he had hinted at what might then happen had left a nameless dread impressed upon her young mind. Somehow, he had been able to make her feel that she was responsible for what had happened. Oh... how could she, at only eleven years of age, feel so helpless and trapped?

Dear mothers and fathers, not only is this story true,[14] but some version of this story has been repeated over and over again in our Plain communities. And it is still happening today. Are we actually helpless to put a stop to this?

In Sarah's case, it took over thirty years, including a troubled marriage and finally an emotional breakdown, before she finally found the courage to tell her story to an understanding counselor. Hard as it is to believe, she had never told anyone before, not even her husband. After all these years of suppressing her true feelings rather than facing what had happened, it was very hard to change. But for Sarah the story ends with victory. She found support from her husband and family, her church and extended community, as well as an understanding mentor/counselor. She started rebuilding her life. Now she is a shining illustration of what the love of God

---

[4] As always, names and details have been changed to protect the identity of the individuals involved.

can do in one person's life. Today her life is an example of the plan of redemption that has been given to mankind.

But the question for us is, why was this thirty-year struggle necessary? What could her parents, the church, and community have done to prevent it? There are many ways in which we can help our children so that stories such as Sarah's need not continue. In today's permissive society we parents have a duty to protect our innocent children by the things that we teach them as they grow. Let us discuss some of the specific things we need to be teaching our children in today's world.

Removing the cloak of secrecy

As Sarah and many other children could have told us over the years, ignorance is not always bliss! Even though there are varying opinions among the Plain communities as to how much and at what age certain facts of life should be discussed with our children, one thing is sure: complete silence on these subjects is not the answer.

We always cringe when we hear parents make mention of having "the talk" with their child. Most of us would not dream of having a "once and done" talk with our children about any other subject, like, for instance, lying. Can you imagine not speaking to your child about always being truthful, and then one day you sit down and talk about "it." Would you somehow expect him to remember this so well that you would never need to mention it again?

No. As soon as a child is old enough to talk and understand what he is saying, we let him know in various ways that we expect him to tell the truth. At three years of age, he may not understand the importance of telling the truth, nor does he need to understand that lying displeases God. All he needs to understand is that Mom and Dad expect him to tell the truth. As children grow older, they may need to be reminded, and as they mature, they may understand bit by bit that lying is not only displeasing to Mom and Dad, but to God as well. Not until they are more mature can they fully understand the importance of why it is good to earn the trust and confidence of our fellow man by always being entirely honest in everything we do.

In the same way, when teaching about the "facts of life," we should not wait until children can fully understand all the facts before teaching them. At a very young age, children should be taught some of the basics, such as where little babies come from. At this age, they may not understand everything. In fact, it may not be appropriate to talk about all the details of reproduction. But as they grow and mature, it is important to teach what is appropriate for their age and understanding.

In the world we live in today, where little is held sacred anymore and all subjects seem to be discussed with equal irreverence, it may be hard to know where to draw the line. Certainly we do not want to follow the ways of the world around us where there is no shame where shame should be. Intimacy is openly displayed and discussed by all. However, it is exactly because of this trend in the popular culture around us, that we need to talk to our children repeatedly at appropriate ages. If we do not do this, one thing is certain: most children will learn of the subject somewhere else. And in many cases, the wrong source of information will do much damage.

Is there any other subject where we would have our children learn the truth of the matter from their peers rather than from their parents?

Naming names

As our children grow, it is important that they learn to express themselves in a way that others can understand them. We teach our children words to express their feelings when they are happy, sad, or angry. We teach them words to ask for help when they need a drink of water or cannot reach something. We also teach children words for their visible body parts, such as an arm, a toe, or nose.

In the same way, it is important that we teach our children names for their private body parts, the parts other people usually don't see. Pretending girls and boys do not have unique body parts, or that it is shameful to mention those body parts, can be very harmful to children. Having mysterious "unmentionables" gives children the idea they need to keep certain things secret and makes them vulnerable to sexual abuse.

> Having mysterious "unmentionables" gives children the idea they need to keep certain things secret and makes them vulnerable to sexual abuse.

Similarly, children are often curious about where babies come from. We could say, "When parents love each other, God often blesses them with a baby. The baby grows inside the mother's body, and when the baby is big enough, it is born so we can all love and care for it."

We don't need to talk about these things at the supper table or at a family gathering. But we can name specific body parts when we're bathing our children or when we are helping them to change clothes. We can certainly use appropriate, descriptive words when our children ask us questions. Parents should decide together how they will answer their children's questions and what words they will use.

Safe secrets, unsafe secrets

What child does not love a secret? Birthday cakes, a gift for mother, or a surprise for their teacher—what fun! Unfortunately most abusers ask children to keep their actions a secret. Sometimes

56

abusers even threaten children about what will happen if they tell. Even if not told to do so, most children will keep the abuse a secret. How can we encourage our children never to keep secrets of things that are not as they should be? What makes this even more important is that, quite often, an abuser is someone whom the child should trust under normal circumstances, someone that the child knows quite well. Because of this, it is very important to explain to children what is a safe secret and what is an unsafe secret.

A safe secret is usually a nice secret, one that will soon be revealed. There are many of these kinds of secrets, and it is usually not hard to think of examples we can tell our children about.

With unsafe secrets, the child is usually instructed to tell no one, not even his or her parents. When teaching children what an unsafe secret is, it is good to use specific examples. Parents must teach their children that under no circumstances should they promise to "never tell anyone." Children should be told often that it is never a safe secret if they are told to keep it a secret when someone did something to them, regardless of who that person is, even if it is someone they know very well, such as a family member.

A good saying for children to learn is, "If a secret is about touching, you should tell your parents."

Sometimes an abuser will say that the child will be hurt or that something terrible will happen if they tell. If children are consistently taught, both by word and example, that it is always safe to confide in their parents, such threats will lose their power.

Good touch, bad touch

As children grow, touch is such an important part of communicating love. But children should be taught at a young age what is a safe touch. A good rule is that any area below the shoulders and above the knees is off limits and if anyone tries to touch them there, this is a "bad touch." Children should be taught it is okay to say "no" to someone, even an adult, if a touch makes them feel uneasy or scared. There is nothing wrong with being very explicit when explaining what areas of the body are safe for others to touch. It is especially important to teach our children that if anyone touches their private parts, they should immediately tell an adult.

When it is okay to say "no"

Most of us will tell our children they should never say "yes" to a stranger who offers to give them a ride. Some parents also tell their children they should never accept gifts from strangers unless their parents or some other adults are with them and say it is okay. This is important and will safeguard them in certain situations. But because so much abuse happens by someone that the child knows, we need to do much more than this.

We teach our children they should be respectful to adults, and this is good and right. However, they should also be taught that it may sometimes be okay to say "no" to an adult, even if it is someone they love.

> ...[children] should also be taught that it may sometimes be okay to say "no" to an adult, even if it is someone they love.

In the booklet, "When to Say No"[15], the example is given:

If your neighbor says, "Come to the barn. I want to show you our puppies."

Tell him, "I'll have to ask Dad or Mom first."

Another example is—

"It is okay to say no when someone grabs and tickles you, even if it's meant for fun. It is okay to say no even to someone you love."

---

[15] *When to Say No.* Weaverland Publications, 2009

It is just as important to teach children that if they need to say no to someone, they should always tell their mother or father right away.

Not only should they be taught to say no if a stranger wants to give them a gift, but if a friend or relative gives them a gift, they should be taught to tell their parents.

> *Elias was at a produce auction with his niece, Christina. A man noticed that Christina was bidding on a box of corn flakes, so he bought it and tried to give it to her. Christina told her uncle who immediately went to speak with the man. The man was very defensive and began talking very fast. Elias just kept asking him why he had done that. Elias learned later this man had done this at other auctions as well. Elias was grateful Christina had told him and wondered if Christina's parents had not had conversations with her about these kinds of situations.*

As we teach our children about specific actions that may be unsafe, about good touch versus bad touch, about safe secrets or unsafe secrets, as well as about it being okay to say no, we are helping to make our neighborhoods be the safe places they should be. On the other hand, if our child comes and tells us about the unsafe actions of a person, we do have a duty to make sure the proper people know about this. Perhaps by doing so we are protecting someone else's child from harm.

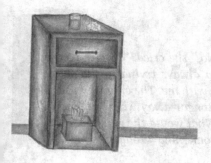

Chapter 6

Getting Help

As Martha lay in bed, curled up in pain, she kept wondering what could be wrong. What could be the cause of so much pain? She vaguely remembered hearing that the symptoms of appendicitis were like this: the low-grade fever, the occasional pain in her lower right side that was getting worse these last days, and now this sharp pain that would not go away.

She cringed when she heard the door quietly open. This would be Sam again, insisting that he should get help for her. Sure enough, his kind eyes clouded with concern, he asked her, "How do you feel?"

Martha refused to answer, turning her head toward the wall. Why did he have to act as if there was something wrong with her? She could take care of herself.

"Martha," came her husband's firm voice. "I am going to take you to the doctor. I've made an appointment for 2 *o'clock this afternoon."*

Instantly Martha reacted. "No," she cried. "I won't go. You can't make me. Why are you always trying to shame me? There's really nothing wrong with me. The only way that I'll go along is if we go to a doctor far away where no one will ever find out that we went. What would the neighbors think if they knew that there was something wrong with me?"

Wearily, Sam sat on the bed beside her. They had been through this before. How could he persuade his wife to go for help before it was too late?

Of course we realize the above story is absurd and could not really be true. But wait a minute. Is it really that far-fetched?

If we slip on the ice and break our arm, we do not hesitate to go to the doctor. If we don't know what to do with our hyper child or what to feed our baby, we turn to a grandparent or aunt or a clinic.

Why then are we so hesitant to seek help if we feel sad all the time or so tired that we want to spend all day in bed, maybe even feel that life is not worth living?

Why, if we cannot seem to keep our anger under control, or a loved one is a threat to those about him, are we so hesitant to invite the help of a minister or mental health professional?

Why, if we suspect a child is being hurt by someone they know do we look the other way? Or if we suspect a youth is being abused, why do we hesitate to speak up?

Getting help does not mean we are weak or helpless or worthless. It actually means we care enough about ourselves and others that we will make the effort to find a person or organization to help keep everyone safe.

> Getting help:
> -Mental illness
> -Depression
> -Abuse situations

Sometimes, like Martha in the story above, we do not go for help because we feel shame. We do no want others to know that we are struggling.

Sometimes we feel we can handle the situation ourselves. Others wouldn't understand anyway.

And sometimes we do not go for help because we do not know where to go.

In this chapter, we would like to talk about how to find help for the various situations and illnesses we may meet up with.

Getting help: MENTAL ILLNESS

Even though this book is about safety and abuse, we would also like to mention getting help for mental illnesses here, as the two are sometimes intertwined. Abuse may happen more frequently in families where one of the parents is battling with mental illness or depression. Getting help in time can vastly improve the other family members' outlook on life and may make the difference so that a child does not feel the need to look for love in all the wrong places.

There are many different types of mental illnesses. In years past, many people with mental illness would be locked away in some institution. While this may not have been ideal, at least it kept the other family and community members safe. Many of us may remember the story of Patrick Henry[16], one of the founding fathers of the United States, who kept his wife locked in his basement for many years. Although he cared faithfully for her, he made sure that she could not escape and that there was nothing in her room with which she could harm herself.

Today, because of discoveries in how mental illnesses work and the development of medications, many people with mental illnesses lead fairly normal lives and do not have to be locked up.

The first step in helping someone with a mental illness is

---

[16] *Sara Shelton Henry: The Wife Patrick Henry kept in the Cellar.* Sheila Phelps Inderbitzen. Outskirts Press, 09 June 2016.

usually to take them to a family doctor. Depending on the extent of the illness, the doctor may refer the individual to a psychiatrist. A psychiatrist is a doctor who is specially trained to work with mental illnesses, both in diagnosing the illness and in prescribing medications. Although not counselors, psychiatrists may sometimes recommend seeing a therapist or counselor, depending on the illness. Some mental illnesses may respond favorably to counseling, while others, such as certain forms of schizophrenia, are often helped very little by counseling. Social workers may also be able to help someone with mental illness and their families to find ways to keep everyone safe.

Then there are some types of mental illnesses that may benefit from a combination of medication and counseling, such as some forms of bipolar disorder. These patients often ride a roller coaster of highs and lows. During parts of this cycle, they may become convinced they no longer need their medication. It is not unusual for these patients to crash numerous times before they discover they really do need to stay on their medications for the long term. Similar to someone who has Type 1 diabetes, they may need to be on medication for the rest of their lives.

Even in today's world where many persons with disabilities are able to lead normal lives, a certain stigma still seems to be connected to mental illness. Sometimes family members are reluctant to get help for a person with the symptoms of mental illness, because, like Martha in the story above, they worry about what others will think. However, we now know that reaching out for help is sometimes the best thing we can do to help someone we love.

Getting help: DEPRESSION

Are you or someone close to you feeling overwhelmed much of the time? Is something bothering you that just doesn't seem to go away? Are you having trouble sleeping? Do you often feel out of control? Or like life is not worth living?

You do not need to face this alone. There is help available.

One of the first places to go for help should be the church ministry. In some areas, there are lay people appointed who may be able to help in such situations. Even if your ministry is not able to help you personally, they may know where to find the help you need.

In cases of serious depression, an evaluation by a mental health professional may be needed. This is especially true if the depression has progressed to the point where someone may be harmed. If the depression is serious enough, hospitalization may be required. But even in the cases where medication becomes necessary, with proper counseling and support from the church and community, the goal would be to resume a normal life apart from lifelong dependence on medication.

If there is reason to believe that a family member is suffering from serious depression, you may need to see a family doctor, who may then refer you to a psychiatrist or therapist.[17] You may also call one of the mental health facilities that are listed in the resources at the end of this book.

In some of our communities, the leadership has reached out to health professionals and learned to identify those who are most accepting of our way of life, and are willing to respect our traditions and faith. We encourage more communities to reach out in this way. There may be professionals in your area who are willing to learn about our way of life, and who would be willing to do whatever they can to help us, while also respecting our faith.

---

[17] We strongly encourage using only psychiatrists, therapists, and social workers who have been approved by the leadership of your church as the training that some of these professionals receive is not friendly to our understanding of the conservative Christian faith. Usually you can trust those mental health centers in our communities that are administered by the Plain community. Some of these are listed in the "Recommended Resources" section at the end of this book.

There are books and other resources that we could suggest to them if they want to learn about our culture. Especially helpful might be Donald Kraybill's book, *Simply Amish* or organizations such as *Dove's Nest,* which offers cultural training to government and other professional agencies.

Getting Help: ABUSE SITUATIONS

As was discussed in earlier chapters, the cry of an abused child may be hard to recognize. An abused child will not usually come right out and tell us they are being abused. Even if they are asked directly, an abused child will most often deny any abuse. It may be more in what they do not say than what they actually say in so many words. Of course, if we have reasonable suspicions of abuse, it should be reported to the proper authorities. In any case, if we suspect abuse, it may be wise to seek the help of those who have been appointed in our communities to work with those situations, including child protection or police.

Over the years, we have encountered many situations where a child finally told an adult about the abuse and they were not believed. Remember, abusers are great manipulators. To us, it may seem quite unbelievable that the accused individual would do anything of the kind. Sadly, many a mother has even punished her child for saying something so unthinkable about a family member, relative, parent, or grandparent.

Often, the abused child is crying for help inside, but no one understands. She has no idea how her actions look to others. To some, she may look like an unmanageable child who wants attention. Because of how troubled she is, her past actions and attitudes may make it seem obvious that she is not to be trusted. So when she finally does tell of the abuse, it may seem like just another of her "shenanigans."

Dear parents and caregivers, if a troubled child mentions any kind of sexual abuse, regardless how unbelievable the story may be, or how much the child's past actions may make you doubt yet another story, **do not ignore it.** Even the most trying child does not make up idle stories with details of sexual misconduct.

Abusers are great manipulators. In many cases they make it appear as if the victim is just as guilty as they are. Quite often they are able to make the victim feel as if it were at least partly their

> If a troubled child mentions any kind of sexual abuse, regardless how unbelievable the story may be, or how much the child's past actions may make you doubt yet another story, **do not ignore it.**

own fault. Because of this many a child has been made to feel guilty for something that they were coerced into. The last thing that such a child needs is to have the adults in their lives tell them, either by words or actions, that we hold them partly responsible.

If a child talks about abuse, either directly or indirectly, we do well to listen carefully. The last thing they need is for us to overreact. The worst thing we can do is to show our agitation or become upset. Remaining calm and carefully asking about it in a matter-of-fact tone of voice will reassure the child that it is safe to discuss the matter. If the child clams up and refuses to say more, it may be better for you to tell him how brave he was to tell you about it, rather than becoming upset and demanding. Then bring the subject up later when the time seems right.

Sometimes a child will disclose abuse to an extended family member, such as a grandparent, aunt, or cousin. We encourage such extended family members to get help from the ministry or a crisis team member outside of the family. It is rare that it will work out in the long run to have extended family members involved too closely.

It is usually not advisable to go alone to confront a person suspected of abuse. Remember, abuse situations usually evolve over time, and in most cases, the abuser is living in denial. Lying about the abuse may be just another little sin on top of the rest of his hidden secrets, and in his mind, it may be justified. Here again, it is advisable to find someone with experience in these situations.

Finding the right help for abuse situations is often not as simple as finding help for depression or mental illness. Many times, depending on the circumstances, we should first go to the home ministry. Even if they cannot solve the situation, they may know where to go for help. There have been circumstances in the past where the home ministry was unable or unwilling to act, and in these situations, we advise to keep looking for help elsewhere.

In many communities, there are crisis teams who have been appointed to help in abuse situations. Many of these have experience and training and can be trusted to handle the situation with the discretion needed for sensitive situations. Some of these teams are listed in the resources at the end of the book. Even if there is no crisis team set up for your community, a crisis team from another community may be willing to help.

Some notes on mandatory reporting: Most states and provinces have specific laws on mandatory reporting of abuse. These vary from state to state, but many of the laws are very similar. A key part of many of these laws is the term, "If you have reasonable cause for suspicion." If mandated reporters have reasonable cause for suspicion that abuse is occurring or has occurred, they are required by law to report it to the appropriate authorities. In the last few years, we have seen the laws on reporting abuse become much more stringent, including the designation on who is a mandated reporter. Generally, a mandated reporter is any health professional, including mental health professionals and therapists, all teachers, and all child care workers. In some states, such as Pennsylvania, the designation includes "an individual paid or unpaid, who, on the basis of the individual's role as an integral part of a regularly scheduled program, activity or service, is a person responsible for the child's welfare." This definition, in those states where it applies, would include private school teachers, Sunday school teachers, as well as all ministry and all child care workers, even if they are not licensed.

The question often comes up, "How can we as Bible-believing people reconcile the command of Matthew 18, 'If thy brother shall trespass against thee, go and tell him his fault between thee and him alone,'[18] with the reporting requirements today?"

The entire issue hinges on the words, "If thy brother shall trespass against thee." What sins would this include?

Perhaps he trespassed by moving the line-fence and thereby taking some of his neighbor's land, or borrowing something and returning it broken, or slandering a brother's name by repeating unkind gossip. There are many ways that a brother can trespass against a brother personally, and in those cases a person needs to go alone to the person who mistreated him and see if they can come to an understanding.

But what about serious sins that are much more than a personal trespass against an individual? Did Jesus also imply that if my brother murdered his neighbor or raped my wife that I would need to go to him and talk with him between me and him alone, and if he hears me, I have gained my brother?

God forbid! Such a sin needs to be reported immediately to the proper civil authorities, who do not carry the sword in vain (Romans 13:1-6). Only then should they be taken to the Church.

Yes, we believe that if a brother has trespassed against us, we should first approach him alone. But if we discover that he has seduced a neighbor's 13-year-old child and ended up violating him or her (either emotionally or physically), we do not believe that Jesus would hold us to the command to keep it "between thee and

---

[18] Matthew 18:15

him alone." Such a brother has not only trespassed against his neighbor, but he has broken the laws of God himself as well as the laws of the land. This is not only a trespass against an individual, but a heinous crime. We are duty bound, both for our brother's sake and for our child's sake (as well as possible future victims), to report him.

Today we know of the terrible hold of sexual addictions. We have seen perpetrators who have been found out, and who "repented" and made their sins right with the church, and life supposedly went on as usual. But life did not go on as usual. The sexual addiction had not been dealt with, and later there were relapses, with more cover-ups, more victims, and more children whose lives were forever changed. This happened because we did not deal with the sin in an appropriate and timely manner.

Our highest goal should be the redemption of the soul that is in bondage. And to find true freedom, the offender needs to take full ownership of his or her iniquity and transgressions as well as his or her civil responsibilities. Civil authority is often a necessary part of breaking the bondage.

We need to acknowledge and recognize the difference between a trespass against a brother that can be taken care of "between thee and him alone," and serious sins that are much more than just a personal trespass.

This is why we feel that it is good and proper and, indeed, necessary to obey the laws on mandated reporting.

The Role of Church Committees

As we have become more aware of abuse among us, many communities have been proactive by appointing special crisis teams to deal with abuse situations that come up within the church community. Some of the names of these teams are: Family Support Team; Conservative Crisis Intervention; Restoration Team; and

Abuse Awareness Team.

See the resources at the end of the book for the contact information of some of these crisis teams in the Conservative Mennonite and Amish communities. Many of these will be open to extending a helping hand if there is no crisis team in your area.

The first role of these teams is to help the family when abuse is discovered. They can help to ensure that the victim is safe and may be able to help the victim find healing through a program or counseling. If the perpetrator is repentant, they may help him find the proper help and counseling to break free from the bondage of addiction. If the law is involved, they may be able to help him through the legal maze. Quite often, they have a working relationship with the local Children and Youth Services (CYS) and other officials who may be involved in the case. In some cases, they may be able to arrange to have some or all of the required counseling done within our own conservative circles. Even if they are not able to have the penalty reduced, they can help provide the support that the abuser and family need over this time

Below is a sample of a statement of purpose of one of these committees.[19]

Conservative Crisis Intervention

Serving the Old Order Mennonite Community

And we urge you, brethren, admonish the unruly, encourage the fainthearted, help the weak, be patient with all men. Thessalonians 5:14

When the Holy spirit dwells within his people they change. The former desires no longer entice them, now their chief aim is to please God.

---

[19] Used by permission of Conservative Crisis Intervention, Lancaster County, Pennsylvania.

Our Vision:

To help Victims become free of their burden and to understand Christ is the way to freedom.

To help Men & Boys get Victory over their bondage of sin. To give men Hope in bondage, that there is hope at the Cross and that Jesus redeemed our sins.

Mission Statement:

To have a core group of Men understand the law and have a good relationship with Children and Youth Agencies, to intercede for our Old Order Mennonite communities battling sexual struggles.

Objectives of the Crisis Center Prevention

To establish a good working relationship with the CYS, District Attorney's and the State Officials.

An organization comprised of persons from the Old Order Mennonite Churches, whose purpose will be to provide assistance and information to members of the afore-mentioned Churches when they are faced with instances of sexual acting out or inappropriate behavior, physical or domestic violence or abuse.

This team will be able to provide assistance in formulating treatment plans for the victims and the abuser who has sexually, physically or emotionally molested or abused others, especially smaller children and minors in churches, and to make sure the <u>victims are safe</u>.

The team will work with the perpetrator and his ministry to make an application to enroll him into a program tailored to his needs and to set up a support group.

The team will also work with the ministry and the perpetrator in developing a probation plan that is directly *linked to the seriousness of the offenses, realizing that the Church will need to satisfy the Law and Children of Youth services. If the offender is a perpetrator, predator, or a pedophile, we would work up a probation letter with rehabilitation and a support group. We would also assist in setting up training for the accountability team if we feel it is needed.*

Team members will be able to provide direction in setting up an accountability team to support the perpetrator and to keep him accountable. We have experienced that these accountability teams are the key to having our rehabilitation programs be successful.

While we know that having the perpetrator receive the proper help to understand his wrongs is a very important step to recovery, we also see the victims of these offenses as needing just as much help or more help. Help to process the abuse, to understand that Jesus can and does restore to wholeness and Purity, to understand Forgiveness, to find their voice, to understand their emotions, to grow and mature as normal teenagers and not carry hurtful baggage into their marriage.

If anyone has any questions or comments please feel free to call at anytime.

Support Groups

It has become an accepted practice in many communities for the church to appoint a separate support group to walk with the family when there has been abuse. This has proven to be a wonderful way to assure that the family receives the support they need during this time. Often the crisis teams can assist in setting up the support group, although it is best if the church leaders make the final selections and approvals for setting up the support group. In most cases we recommend that a separate support group be set up to work with the abuser if he or she is repentant.

When a support group has been set up, it is best for the extended family to step back. If they have concerns, they should bring them to the support group, rather than talk directly to the family about it. Letting the family know you care and are praying for them but that you have given the direct responsibility over to the support group can do wonders for the family that is being supported.

Below are support group guidelines that are being used in many communities.[20]

SETTING UP A SUPPORT GROUP

When setting up a support group, it is important to choose couples (individuals) who are solidly grounded in the church and the community. Special effort should be made to choose only such as are team players, who know how to work together as a team. It does not work out well if one committee member does all the talking, and the rest just tag along for the ride.

We advise that the one(s) to be supported be given the chance to choose a couple they trust and are comfortable with, although the ministry has the right to insist their choice meet the criteria mentioned above. The ministry should then pick the next couple, and then those two couples should choose the third couple. All support group members should be approved by the ministry, and the ministry should ask them to serve.

When the chosen persons have agreed to serve, one or two meetings should be held by the support group alone to get acquainted and to get everyone on the same page as how

---

[20] Used by permission of Conservative Crisis Intervention, Lancaster County, Pennsylvania.

best to help. This is a good time to fill the chairman position. If the deacon or other ministry wishes to attend the first meeting, they may appoint the chairman. Also one should be appointed to keep notes or minutes of every meeting.

It is of utmost importance that the group work together in unity and harmony. Otherwise more harm may be done than good.

GOALS FOR A SUPPORT GROUP

The main goal of the support group is to support, encourage, and help to make good decisions in the issues that are facing the people they are helping. And to keep them accountable to their goals and accountability agreement, in a kind and reasonable way.

Meetings should be held on a regular schedule, as often as the support group feels it is necessary, perhaps every 2 weeks. We recommend starting the meeting with a song and a silent prayer. Then the one appointed to lead should start the meeting and keep it orderly, making sure that people wait on their turn to speak. No personal attacks should be tolerated. The ones being supported should be encouraged to speak openly about any problems or issues they would like to discuss. This is an important part of the meeting. As they learn to trust the support group it becomes easier to share problems or concerns before they get out of hand.

If any differences or problems arise, it is the support group's duty to consider the issue and find a solution. Any minor issues can be worked out right at the meeting. However, major decisions should not be so hastily made. It is better to discuss the issue, then say you need time to consider the problem. Then the support group can meet alone to make the final decision. If it is a church issue, you should go to the ministry for advice. Everyone involved should then cooperate with the advice or decision that is made.

When there is not much to discuss at the meetings, a suggestion is to use a book such as "One Anothering" or "Smoother Journey" and read a chapter, taking turns to read a paragraph, and just have an open and interesting discussion. Hopefully, everyone will look forward to meeting and sharing together in love and Christian fellowship.

In some situations, it may be good to have support group women talk alone with the wife occasionally, and the same with the men, to get to the root of private issues. If there are grown children, it is good to meet with them alone to consider their views.

FINANCIAL COMMITTEES

If money matters are part of the problem, all income and expense records should be open for the support group, so they may help financially or give advice. In serious financial cases, it may be necessary to appoint one of the support group members as a legal power of attorney, and to at least temporarily take over the checkbook and all financial decisions. It is recommended that in this case the supported couple sign a financial agreement.

INVOLVEMENT OF OTHERS

All things should be kept confidential, so all may learn to trust each other and openly share. Then all others – parents, friends, family – back off unless the support group asks for the ministry's help. Family may visit and be friendly, but should leave all problems to the support group. If family members disagree with any decisions or actions, it is important they talk to the support group alone, rather than directly to the supported persons.

Sometimes the question comes up, "When should a support group disband?" Our answer is, "Don't be in too much of a hurry." As the supported ones learn to use what they have learned, the time may come when they would desire to be on their own. At this time, it may be better to back off a little at a time, rather than completely disbanding. As long as the supported ones desire to meet, the support group has a duty to keep supporting them. If the supported ones are sure they no longer need support, but the support committee sees there is still a need, it may be good to get the ministry involved with the decision on whether to disband.

Chapter 7

Role of Social Services

"Andrew, with all you've been through the last couple days, this is the last thing you need!" Amos spoke forcefully, as he faced his brother. "Now, if it were me, I would tell them in no uncertain terms that I've suffered enough, and they have no business intruding."

Andrew shook his head in puzzlement. "But I have nothing to hide. If there's something we should do to make our home safer, I guess I'm willing to listen..."

"You don't understand." Amos cut him off. "Those agents are out to get us. They are going to cite you for anything that doesn't come up to their expectations. We Plain people have different standards than they do, and they don't understand this. They expect us to conform to their idea of how to raise children. If you allow them into your house, they are likely to take your children from you. Our children are viewed as underprivileged if we don't have all the modern conveniences and entertainments that they take for *granted. If we allow them into our homes, we are just asking for trouble. And besides, we live in America. Here we have some rights, and we have a right to decide who we want to allow into our homes."*

Andrew slowly shook his head again. "Well, thanks for the advice. It gives us something to think about, anyway."

Later, after Amos had left, Andrew discussed his brother's attitude with his wife. They both agreed that losing their 5-year-old son was hard enough to cope with, without having some agency watching their every move now, regardless how well-meaning they were. However, their views of how to respond to the county's Children and Youth Services (CYS) was certainly not the same as Amos'.

"My feeling," said Andrew slowly, "is that the people from CYS who are coming tomorrow are just as human as we are. They have a job to do, and when they come to interview a grieving family, the last thing they want to do is make it harder for us. But, if we resist them, they still have their job to do. In fact, the harder we make it for them, the more reason they have to be suspicious."

His wife wiped away a tear. "I know, but it's so hard to open my heart to strangers right now. I just wish they would leave us alone."

Andrew nodded understandingly. "I know. But let's just wait and see what the day brings."

As Andrew let his mind go over the events of the last two weeks, he had to remind himself again that God had allowed all this to happen. It was hard not to blame himself for allowing an accident like this to happen. He also knew how some of the neighbors felt. In fact, one of them had voiced the opinion that since Jeremy had been mentally limited and needed more care than their other children, the parting would not be as hard. *Obviously, he doesn't know what he's talking about,* thought Andrew. As any parent with a mentally challenged child would understand, the fact that Jeremy was "special" did not make him any less loved than their other children. In fact, if it was possible, out of all their children they had a "special" love for him. One of the reasons finding him in the farm pond was so hard to accept was the realization that Jeremy would not have been able to understand the danger. Andrew needed to remind himself again that God's will was supreme and His grace was sufficient, even in circumstances such as these.

Much to Andrew's relief, the visit from the Children and Youth Services was not at all what they had feared. The woman who came out was very sympathetic. She had lost a son herself, and Andrew and his wife could feel true empathy as she asked them to share their story. She explained that it was her duty to interview parents after an accident like this, and she had the best interests of all involved. She politely asked permission to go through the house, and especially wanted to walk down to the pond in the meadow where Jeremy's body had been found. She specifically asked about safety measures that might have kept Jeremy from wandering down to the pond unattended. Andrew and his wife tried to be open and honest, and because of the understanding attitude of the social worker, it was easy to be so. In the end, she assured them that she would recommend they should not be charged with negligence. However, she felt the agency might require a better fence and gates that were child proof, so a similar accident might not occur in the future.

Cooperating with Social Services

To many of us, the thought of an investigation by the CYS may be terrifying. But in most cases, as Andrew and his wife discovered, they really have our best interests at heart. And, as Andrew

> The thought of an investigation by the CYS may be terrifying, but in most cases they really have our best interests at heart.

correctly surmised, resisting only implies we have something to hide, while being completely open and honest will usually make so that they will try to work with us the best they can.

On the other hand, if there is ongoing abuse, they do have the authority to enforce any changes that may be required to bring safety and justice to the situation. As Paul wrote two thousand years ago, "For rulers are not a terror to good works, but to the evil. Wilt thou then not be afraid of the power? Do that which is good, and thou shalt have praise of the same."[21]

This is exactly what we have discovered over the years. The social service personnel that our crisis teams have worked with have often been extremely grateful for our willingness to work with them. Occasionally, they have had words of praise for the plain people, even when encountering situations of abuse. This was illustrated in a case where a therapist, who was working with a victim in the Plain community, had called a meeting with the victim's family and the social worker assigned to the case. It so happened that not many plain people lived in this county at the time. At the meeting, the social worker made mention of the fact that this was the first meeting in her many years of experience where she could feel this level of support for the victim and his family. Her words to the parents were, "Around this table, we have 11 chairs that are filled with people who care. In most of the situations we work with, these chairs are empty. No one is in them except the lonely person we are working with."

[21] Romans 13:3

A number of times parents have expressed their fears that the social services do not understand our culture and are only too ready to separate families and take our children and place them in foster homes that are not sensitive to our ways. This fear is understandable as there were a few situations where this happened years ago. However, the climate has changed in most social service

> The climate has changed in most social service agencies today, and much emphasis is put on being culturally sensitive.

agencies today, and much emphasis is put on being culturally sensitive. The Plain people are not the only group with a unique culture. There are many minority groups in the U.S. and Canada that the social services need to work with, such as Vietnamese, Hispanic, and Native American. They are doing their best to be sensitive to the culture of each of these groups as well.

In fact, it has been many years since we have heard of the Children and Youth Services coming in and forcefully removing children without finding other Plain family homes to place them in.

The Structure of Social Services

Every state has a department of social services that is tasked with enforcing child abuse laws. The laws on identifying and responding to abuse vary somewhat from state to state and from province to province, but mostly they are similar. In many states, each county has their own department of social services, but each county within that state has the same laws they need to abide by.

These laws define abuse and also what steps need to be taken when a child is suspected to be a victim of abuse. The law has specific criteria that must be met before social services will investigate and even more specific criteria before they will remove a child from a home. Although each state's definitions and criteria are different, each case must go before a judge before a child can be removed from a family for more than a couple of days.

The role of social services, as outlined in law, is not only to investigate possible child abuse, but also to provide assistance to families. In a way, their concerns are very similar to ours, in that they are working to keep children safe. And like us, they really want children to stay in their own families. Social services may suggest services such as medical care, counseling, and parenting classes, and they can make useful referrals for housing and other services for those who need additional support. However, because they are often aware of the Plain people's extensive support system within the church, they may allow us to use our own internal support system wherever appropriate.

One government worker would likely investigate the possible abuse, and if the abuse is confirmed, the case may be referred to an ongoing worker for further services. Both workers will have supervisors who must sign off each step of the way. Depending on the nature of the case, a judge may also be involved.

> It is important that we cooperate with social services when they are doing these interviews.

After receiving a call about a child possibly being abused and the report meets the criteria, the worker will first try to make contact with the child. The worker will ask the child questions about who she lives with and if she is scared of anyone, or being hurt by anyone, or any questions that may be necessary to determine if the child is safe or is being abused. The worker will then seek to interview the parents and any other people who may have information about the situation or who the alleged abuser(s) might be. Sometimes, depending on the age of the child, they may need to find a translator who can speak our language fluently. This is not unusual, as they have other minority groups, such as Spanish-speaking families, for whom they also use translators.

It is important that we cooperate with social services when they are doing these interviews. We need to answer their questions as thoroughly as we can. It is okay to let them know if we don't understand a certain question. It is also okay to let them know if we want someone else present for the interview, such as our spouse, a minister, or perhaps another advocate. In communities where there are crisis teams, it is appropriate to ask one of them to accompany us. The worker may know very little about our way of life, so we may need to explain why we want to involve other people.

Social services are bound by strict rules about confidentiality. They cannot include other people in their interviews without specific written permission from you. You may need to tell them you are willing to sign a "release of information" document for each individual who is to accompany you. If you decide to sign a release of information form for the crisis team that is working with you, the agency will be able to discuss the case with the team. This will often allow the team to help you more effectively.

Many social workers have a hard time understanding that many of us Plain people rarely show emotion in public. Most of us will do our grieving in the privacy of our homes. We have been taught to be stoic and to maintain control of our emotions in our interactions in public, such as when we are questioned by "English" social workers or reporters. Therefore, to a social worker who is not familiar with our way of life, it may seem we really don't care when our children are hurt or killed. How can we let them know we are grieving just as much as anyone else, even though we do not tend to show our emotions?

Social services may be uncertain how to help us find the services we need. We can tell them about doctors or clinics we are comfortable going to.

For the Sake of a Child

While it will likely be upsetting for us to have social services visit us, whether it is once or many times, remember they are normal people too, and they are just following rules. We both have one big thing in common: **we all want our children to be safe.**

oster Care & Adoption

Lydia's hands trembled as she signed her name. She looked up at the clock on the wall above the austere-looking guard sitting behind the large metal desk, then wrote down "1:16 p.m." The guard said gruffly, "Okay, take a seat, and we'll call you when someone's available to take you back." Slowly Lydia walked over to the hard-backed bench along the bare wall and sat down. Another wait. Getting in to visit someone in this prison was quite a process. Who would have thought that she, Lydia Burkholder, at 64 years of age, would be coming by herself to visit someone in the state prison?

The minutes ticked on as she sat on the uncomfortable bench. Her mind traveled back to that morning almost 16 years ago when they had first seen little Denise.

Bertha had been the first to see the social worker's car coming in the lane. Bertha, their only child who had such a heart for children and babies. It was Bertha, their dear 10-year-old daughter, who a few years earlier had begged that they consider becoming foster parents. And now it was Bertha who bounced out on the sidewalk to meet Pam, the social worker, and the little girl who she was trying to coax out of the car. This was not the first child Pam had brought out to their house although the others had been younger and had usually been with them for only a short time. When she called to tell them she was coming out with 6-year-old Denise, she had mentioned that this was a little girl who needed lots of love.

As Lydia watched, she saw Pam was not having any luck in persuading the little girl to leave the safety of the car. She saw Bertha bending down to talk with another person in the car. Finally, Bertha climbed into the car herself and sat beside the little girl. Slowly Pam walked around to the back of the car, opened the trunk, retrieved several bags, and then headed toward the house by herself. Several times, she looked anxiously back toward the car before she reached the house. Lydia held the door open for Pam who stepped inside and set the bags on the floor and then sat heavily on a chair at the kitchen table. "Well," she sighed, "I'm hoping you can connect with this child. God knows what she has been through in her short life already. She just doesn't seem to respond to anybody or trust anybody." She shook her head slowly. "I happened to think of your daughter. She seems to have a way with children, and I thought perhaps she can connect with her if anybody can. Remember to keep an eye on her. She's already run off twice. I'm hoping that getting her out of the city was a move in the right direction."

Pam sat, looking out the window. Finally, she turned back to Lydia. "You have no idea how good you have it out here in the country. I just wish we had more stable homes like yours to place children in. And it's so hard to find homes nowadays where the mother is at home instead of having a job." Slowly she got up from her chair. "Well, I guess I better go out and see if we can get that little girl out of my car *before I leave." Lydia and Pam headed back out the door in time to see Bertha and a little wisp of a girl with black hair heading around the corner of the house toward the backyard. Pam just stood there watching them until they disappeared, then said hurriedly, "Well, I think now would be a good time to leave. I'll be in contact tomorrow." And with that she was gone.*

Lydia moved around on the bench trying to find a comfortable position, then glanced again at the clock above the guard's head. That minute hand hardly seemed to move at all. How long would she need to sit here? Again, her mind traveled back, this time to a few weeks after the social worker had brought Denise to their home.

"Mom, what can we try next?" Bertha sat dejectedly at the breakfast table facing her parents. "Denise doesn't seem to want to do anything. And yet if we don't do something with her, she gets into all kinds of trouble."

Lydia and her husband David sat there in silence for a few moments. Finally, David spoke up. "Don't give up. Mom and I can't seem to get through to her either, and at least she's responding a bit more than she did at first." He looked kindly at their daughter and smiled. "I guess we need to get more books to look at. At least that's one thing she'll allow you to do with her."

Lydia nodded encouragingly, "Let's keep trying."

As Lydia mulled over the last few weeks, she wondered why their little foster child had built such a wall around herself. Perhaps it was because she had experienced rejection so often and wished to protect herself from any more hurts. Likely she was not conscious of what she was doing, or why, and that made it hard to get through to her. How her heart must be crying out for love! But at the same time, she resisted any overtures with all her being. How often in the past, when she had allowed someone to come close to her, had she been hurt?

When Lydia thought back to the day Denise first arrived, she realized that even that day had likely felt like just another rejection to the little girl. She had refused to open her heart to Pam, yet when she came back and found the social worker's car gone, she had felt abandoned once more and had retreated into a shell. For the rest of that day, no one could draw her out of that shell.

Although some days were better than others, Denise seemed not to have any self-control. She would purposely destroy something, or torture a little kitten, and when she was discovered, her eyes would open wide in terror. She screamed and kicked and struggled if anyone so much as tried to touch her. As Lydia thought back over the last few weeks, she realized that she and David had not actually held Denise yet. She resisted any kind of touch from adults, and would shrink back if anyone reached out for her, and she vehemently resisted being held. The only person that she allowed to hold her was Bertha, and that only when she was telling her a story out of one of her beloved books.

They all looked up as they heard footsteps on the stairs coming down from the upstairs bedroom. The door opened and Denise stood there, sleepy-eyed and disheveled. She looked at them awhile then headed over toward the table, making a large detour around Lydia and David. Then, taking her chair that stood beside Lydia, she struggled to move it toward Bertha. Finally, when she had moved it over against Bertha's chair and as far away from David as possible, she climbed up on it. Bertha looked across the table at her parents, and even though she didn't say anything, it was easy to see that her heart was soaring.

Lydia's eyes filled with tears as she remembered Pam's words, "Your daughter seems to have a way with children, and I thought perhaps she could connect with her if anybody can."

Some weeks later Denise gave them their first real scare. They had done their best to keep their eye on her. The last few days she had seemed more at home and relaxed, although they all realized this was likely temporary at best. When they were ready to eat supper that evening, they realized that nobody had seen Denise lately. At first, they had not been greatly alarmed. They looked all through the house and in all the places where they knew that she liked to hide.

Finally, when they saw her little footprints in the muddy field lane behind the barn, they realized she must have run away. David had gone across the road to ask his brother and his extended family to help in the search, and they had gone through the fields in organized groups. A little later, it started to rain lightly, and it was a bedraggled group that kept on in the search. David and Lydia were wrestling with the decision on whether or not to call the police to help look for her.

Then as they were going through one of the cornfields and had just reached the end by the creek, almost a half a mile away from their home, Lydia saw one of the neighbor boys motion to her. She hurried over and there, crouched down between the rows of corn, was Denise, wet, bedraggled and miserable. Once again, her eyes had that terrified look, and Lydia thought fleetingly that if she reached out for her, she would probably start screaming and kicking. How she wished that Bertha were here, but she had gone in the opposite direction with another group of searchers.

Slowly Lydia crouched down beside her, and started talking. "Oh, Denise," she said, "Are you ready to come home? You must be cold and miserable." She just stayed there beside her for a few minutes. The rest of the group discreetly moved away, allowing them to be by themselves. Anyway, they were ready to head back home, their duty now done. They were only too glad to notify the others that the lost had been found. Finally Lydia reached out and slowly put her arm around Denise. Denise recoiled and pushed her away slightly, but then slowly allowed herself to be drawn in. As Lydia pulled the little girl's cold body close to herself, Denise stiffened, but eventually she allowed Lydia to pick her up and carry her.

As Lydia headed back toward home, she was glad for once that Denise was such a little wisp of girl and small for a 6-year-old. It started to rain in earnest then, and wonder of wonders, Denise actually snuggled close to her as they headed back. They met others of the search group, but when they offered to carry Denise part of the way, she shook her head. By the time they made it back to the house, Lydia's arms felt as if they were ready to fall off, but she would not have given up the feeling of that little girl snuggled up close to her heart for anything in the world.

Lydia had hoped this would be some kind of magical breakthrough, but it was not to be. Even though Denise no longer actively avoided her, she never again allowed herself to be held like she had that evening.

Lydia looked up as several more people came in and walked over to the guard to ask about visiting someone in the prison. They too were told to sign in and that he would call them when someone was available to take them back. The elderly man with this group asked impatiently how soon this would be. The guard answered shortly without looking up, "We go back once an hour on the hour." Lydia looked up at the clock: 1:48 p.m. Well, perhaps it wouldn't be too much longer. As she shifted on the bench, her mind traveled back once more, this time to their next experience with the runaway.

"David," Lydia exclaimed, "I heard someone at the door."

David looked up from untying his shoes. "Are you sure? I didn't hear anything." However, he dutifully stood up without retying his shoes and shuffled out through the kitchen toward the front door. Lydia watched anxiously as he unlocked the door and peered out into the darkness of the moonless night. Suddenly she saw his shoulders stiffen, and she heard him exclaim, "Denise, what are you doing here?"

Denise? Lydia's mind whirled. Denise was living 40 miles away with her birth mother at this time. They had been in the process of adopting Denise when her mother decided to intervene. Ever since she had appeared on the scene two years earlier, Denise had had a love/hate relationship with her birth mother. She was painfully aware that her mother had abandoned her at two years of age, and even though she had no memories of this, she keenly felt the rejection.

So naturally, when her mother suddenly reappeared in her life eight years later, Denise had a hard time forgiving or accepting her. And yet she had that normal desire of a child to have her mother's approval. That innate, almost fierce desire for approval had disrupted the uneasy peace that had finally settled on them as she became comfortable in David and Lydia's home. As Denise had matured, the shell around her heart had slowly softened, and she seemed to have less fear of rejection the longer she stayed at their home. She still recoiled from any physical touch, but her fits of screaming and reacting violently had long since ceased. For a while, she had called Lydia "Mom," but after her birth mother's first contact, she had refused to call her anything except "Lydia."

After her mother's first visit, Denise had experienced a roller coaster of emotions. Sometimes she rejected her mother and refused to talk to or about her. At other times she tried her best to be just like her. Finally, Denise's mother had persuaded her and had won the agency's approval to have Denise come and live with her.

Of course, it had broken David and Lydia's hearts. Would everything they had tried to teach Denise these last five years now have been in vain?

"Denise, come on in," she heard David say again. Quickly, Lydia hurried out to the kitchen. There in the doorway stood Denise. She had always been small for her age, and now at 12 years of age, she still looked like a little girl. A pang went through Lydia's heart as she saw how bedraggled she looked. How much she looked just like she had that day out in the cornfield. Her eyes held that same terrified look they had come to know so well over the years. She had obviously been wearing the same ragged clothes for several days. Lydia wondered fleetingly what that look in her eyes was all about, and then suddenly her mother heart knew. It was her old fear of rejection. Without a second thought, she reached out her arms, but Denise, true to form, shrank back, avoiding her touch. Lydia noticed that she was shivering. Small wonder, as she did not have nearly enough clothes on for the current weather.

"Come sit at the table," Lydia said in a no-nonsense tone of voice. "I'll make you some hot chocolate."

Denise walked obediently over to the kitchen table and sat down while Lydia bustled about preparing the hot drink for her. It was not till the hot chocolate had warmed her and *she had stopped shivering that they were finally able to talk with her. She admitted that she had run away. "Because," she said in a monotone, "the police came and took my mother away." And then she said the words that warmed Lydia's heart for months to come. "So I decided to come home."*

There was a long silence, then David said huskily, "Well, I believe it's about bedtime. We got a pair of little boys in your old room right now, but for this night, you can sleep in the spare room, next to Bertha's room. Won't she be surprised tomorrow."

And the little girl who had never really cried without throwing a screaming temper tantrum actually got tears in her eyes at these words.

Even though it was late, as soon as Denise was in bed, they called the social services agency and confirmed that, indeed, Denise's mother had been picked up by the police once again, and now worried about her welfare, Denise was to be placed in a foster home. David and Lydia had immediately made a formal request to have Denise live with them again, and the request had been granted.

Denise had lived with them for another four tumultuous years before leaving to live with her mother yet again. This time, she had not come back, even though, as they had found out later, her mother had spent yet another stint in prison. It was now almost two years since they last had any word of Denise. Then, just a few weeks ago, they had received a letter from her. What a shock to see that it came from the state prison. How sad to see that Denise was following in her mother's footsteps.

What could Lydia do? David had recently lost his battle with cancer and she now lived alone, although Bertha and her husband lived just across the road.

"Lydia Burkholder." Lydia jerked out of her reverie. She looked over at the guard behind his desk. A young woman, with unnatural looking blond hair and arms covered with tattoos, was standing beside his desk. Lydia struggled to her feet after sitting on the hard bench for so long, and the young-looking woman walked toward her.

"OK, we're ready to go back," she said in a hoarse voice that did not at all match her young looks. "Who do you want to see?"

"Denise Dawn Mohler," Lydia said uncertainly.

The woman glanced at some paperwork in her hands. "OK, we need to go through the metal detector first. Can I look into your purse?" In spite of her hoarse voice, she seemed kind enough. Taking a quick look into the purse, she placed it on the table beside the metal detector. She turned her attention to Lydia's shoes and told her to take them off before she walked the metal detector. A red light came on and a buzzer sounded. The young-looking guard looked exasperated as she glanced at the pins in Lydia's clothes and covering. Abruptly she gave back her shoes and purse and waved her on. Lydia waited uncertainly while several others went through the safety procedures.

Finally, they were all ready and they followed the guard down a long passageway. Then they passed through a door that needed to be opened by a separate guard, before entering a noisy room that was humming with the sound of many voices. Lydia was told to find a seat and wait till they brought Denise in. What a shock this room was after the quiet and austere surroundings they had been walking through. The guard made her way up to a raised platform where she joined another guard at a desk that was placed at *a vantage point where they could see everyone in the room. The rest of the room was filled with sets of chairs and low tables which were all securely fastened to the concrete floor. Most of the seats were occupied by small groups of people visiting with each other. Lydia spotted one set of chairs that was still unoccupied, and slowly she made her way over to one of the chairs and sat down, glancing tentatively around the room. No one seemed to notice her.*

As she looked around, she slowly became aware that the women with the dull orange jump suits were the prisoners and the others were their visitors. What a sad sight. All types and ages of women in orange suits were visiting with those who had come to see them. At a table close to her sat a man who reminded her of her younger brother, Sylvan. He was talking animatedly with an orange-suited woman whom she guessed to be his wife, although it was hard to guess these women's ages in their strange attire.

Behind them at another table sat a woman, obviously a mother, holding a young child of perhaps three years of age while a slightly older child clung to her side. A man whom she guessed to be the father tried to keep the children calmed down. Right next to them was a young woman with an elderly couple who could have been her parents or grandparents. They were talking to her, but she appeared not to hear them.

Tears came to Lydia's eyes as she looked around at all the women who appeared to be from many backgrounds. Each one of these would have a story to tell, she thought to herself. How did they come to be in this place? How long did they need to stay? What chance did they have to start over once they were released?

Out of the corner of her eye, she noticed another orange-suited woman walking down the aisle toward her. It was not until the woman stopped right next to her that Lydia looked up and suddenly realized that it was Denise.

Lydia tried to get up, but the shock of seeing Denise in her orange suit, looking so much like the rest of the prisoners, made her legs feel like jelly. Of course that is how she would look. She should have known it, but to her Denise was still the young girl who had left them five years ago. Finally, she got to her feet.

She had no reason to do what she did next. All her experiences with Denise should have taught her that she would not welcome any emotional displays. But without thinking what she was doing or even being aware of it, she reached out her arms. Unbelievably, Denise fell into her arms and actually hugged her. It was so unexpected, and Lydia could not stop the tears that coursed down her cheeks. "Oh, Denise," she whispered above the noise of the room. "How I wish I could pick you up and carry you home like I did that time when you were a little girl and got lost in the cornfield."

Lydia noticed that Denise's body was shaking, and it took a few moments for her to realize that Denise was crying. Great sobs shook the girl's body. It was as if a dam had burst and all the emotions she had kept locked up inside her were being released.

"Oh, Mom," she said after she had gotten control of herself. "I was so afraid you wouldn't come."

Had this girl who had held everyone at arm's length all these years actually called her "Mom" again?

"Of course I came," said Lydia. "It wasn't easy, but as soon as I got your letter, I knew that I was going to come. I had to get Edward, Bertha's husband, to help me through the maze

of regulations to get in here." She paused then and looked at Denise. "There's something different about you. What is it?"

"Oh, it's this terrible orange suit. I just hate it," said Denise lightly.

"No, no, I'm not talking about your clothes. It's your face, or something about your eyes. I don't know what it is."

Denise studied her hands that were now folded on the table before her. Finally she looked up. "Well," she said slowly, almost sheepishly, "maybe I am different." She paused so long that Lydia almost thought she had forgotten to go on, then said, "It's a long story, and I want to tell you the whole story sometime. But I can tell you a little about it now. You see, when I came in here, I was terribly bitter at life, at you, at the social workers, at my birth-mom and dad, and at any authority in my life. My roommate was just as bitter, and we often rehearsed all the wrongs that had been done to us. And then one day, she found God. And you know, she really changed. She no longer cursed and swore or yelled at us. She did what she could to make our lives better in here. She really wanted to do better, and even though it was a slow change, she never gave up. And after a while I started to realize something. She had grown up on the street, and had every right to be bitter and hateful. She had never known anything else. She had never been taught right from wrong as I had been. And here she was the one that was making this change. On the other hand, I had every chance to be the better person. I had grown up, at least most of my life that I can remember, with good teachings and a dear mom and dad who would have done anything to help me find the right road in life. I had the teachings, the guidance, and most of all your prayers. And I knew without a doubt that you were still praying for me. All those teachings you gave me as I was growing up in your home came back to me. I had plenty of time to think, and as I watched my friend struggling faithfully on, in spite of her background, I finally knew what I needed to do. I know it took too long, but finally I came back to God."

There was another long pause. Suddenly Lydia noticed the rest of the people in the room were still there, still talking and wrapped up in their own worlds, as if nothing had changed. But for her, so much had changed. The room was much brighter. The feeling of happiness that wanted to bubble out and over her heart made it almost unbelievable to her that the rest of the world could go on as though nothing had happened. She looked back at Denise and said, almost breathlessly, "Oh, Denise, I am so glad. I believe this is the happiest day of my life! It has been worth it all."

On the way home, Lydia only half heard the chatter of her talkative neighbor who had offered to drive her to the prison. Her mind was still back in that prison with Denise. How long had she said she would still be in that horrible prison? Perhaps another six months or up to a year? Lydia knew it would seem like a long time to a young girl. Before Lydia left, Denise had asked for help with some of the questions she and her roommate were struggling with. Lydia had promised to write. And she had assured Denise that she would come back, perhaps with one of the ministers and his wife, and of course, sometime she would bring Bertha along. This would be the beginning of a long journey for Denise, and she prayed that she would not give up or grow weary. Hopefully with the support from home, she could remain faithful.

As Lydia let her mind roam back over the last 20 years since they had decided to become foster parents, she thought again of all the times when they had wondered if it was worth it. Her heart sang at the realization that it was worth it all...after all.

For those of us who have grown up in conservative Christian families, we take it for granted that we are there for each other. If there is a fire, a large hospital bill, or a death in the family, we have the confidence our community will step up and provide the help and support that is needed. The world around us looks at a barn raising after a fire as a peculiar event, as if it were something unusual that people still help each other in this way. We simply take it for granted that this is our normal Christian duty, and if "one member suffer, all the members suffer with it; or one member be honoured, all the members rejoice with it."[22]

Truly, we have been richly blessed above all that we deserve. We have a heritage that we would not trade for anything in the world. And we may well wonder how it has happened that God has blessed us with such a heritage when there are so many around us who are growing up without a moral compass.

Some of us may have a desire to reach out to those who are less fortunate. We will look for ways to show forth the love of God, realizing we live not only to ourselves but also to others.

One of the ways to do this is by providing foster care for children who have been removed from their homes. These last years, we have seen many families in Plain communities across America reach out in this way. Many families find this to be a life-changing experience, both for the foster children who they care for, as well as for themselves and their own families.

Foster care is temporary care for children while social services offers help to the children's parents. Many times the children can eventually return home, sometimes within days or weeks, or sometimes within months or even years.

There are many reasons a child may be put into foster care. The parents may need help with a mental illness or substance abuse or may need to serve a prison term. Sometimes the children are removed because of abuse. Whatever the reason, the children need

[22] 1 Corinthians 12:26

a lot of love. Do we have love to share?

There are even times these children are candidates for adoption. The foster family often has the first opportunity to adopt and can become the child's "forever family."

Becoming a foster home does invite social services into our homes and, to some extent, the family of the foster child. Social workers will visit us, sometimes unannounced, to make sure the child is doing okay. They may assist with taking the child to visit the birth parents or to appointments, or we may be asked to do this ourselves. Depending on the child's age, the child may attend public school.

In order to become a foster home, we will need to complete training and have a home study. Sometimes it may become necessary for us to inform and educate social services about our faith, culture, and way of life. They will expect us to follow many rules about the child's care. One of these requirements is that there is to be no physical discipline.

Many of these children respond well to the love and care we lavish upon them. The state financially compensates foster parents and provides assistance in meeting any special needs the child may have, but the real rewards are not of this world.

At the same time, we need to be aware that not all children will respond as we would wish them to. Some children, like Denise in the story, have experienced abuse or rejection, and it may take time to connect. In the end, most adoptive parents would agree with Lydia that, in spite of all the tears and trials they experience, it is "worth it all."

We may also wish to learn about adopting a child. Many children are waiting for families to adopt them. Some of these are babies. Others may be toddlers or school age children. Some of them have siblings, and they need to be adopted together. Some have physical or emotional disabilities that need special care.

Even if we are not in a position to become foster or adoptive parents, we may be able to offer support to such children and to the families who have taken in these children. What an incredible way to positively affect children for the rest of their lives! Truly the rewards are "out of this world."

Appendix A

Recommended Books

Child Protection and Safety Concerns. (Ephrata, PA: Eastern Mennonite Publications)

Child Training. Joseph Stoll (Aylmer, ON: Pathway Publishers)

Healing from Sexual Sin. (Topeka, IN: Healing Journey)

Holding Out Hope: Mental Health for Plain Communities. Dr. Tony Byler, Rachel Stauffer, and David Byler (Morgantown, PA: Masthof Press)

Let the Children Come: Preparing Faith Communities to End Child Abuse and Neglect. Jeanette Harder (Scottdale, PA: Herald Press)

Sacred Subjects. Amish Ministers (Aylmer, ON: Pathway Publishers) (eight booklets to help parents explain the "sacred subjects" to their children, and how to keep themselves pure)

The Doorway to Hope for the Hurting, Struggling and Discouraged: Unlocking the Door to Hope, You Can Be the Key. (The Sewing Circle: Fort Wayne, IN) (topic: domestic violence)

When to Say "No." Martha Ann Shirk (Ephrata, PA: Weaverland Publications)

Appendix B

Recommended Resources

Mental Health and Psychiatric Services, sponsored by the Plain communities:

• Plain Community Clinic, 243 Butler Road, Lebanon, PA 17042; (717) 989-8661

• Parochial Medical Center, 1065 West Main Street, New Holland, PA 17519; (717) 556-0702

• Green Pastures, 243 Butler Road, Lebanon, PA 17042; (717) 279-2798

• Spring Haven Counseling Center, 15550 Durstine Road, Dundee, OH 44624; (330) 359-6100

• Rest Haven, 225 Lakeview Drive, Goshen, IN 46526; (574) 536-4957

• Woodside Rest, 15550 Durstine Road, Dundee, OH 44624; 330-465-7506 (*for men and women*)

Residential Counseling Centers (by the Plain people):

• Beams of Mercy, 12764 Mount Zion Road, Versailles, MO 65084; (573) 378-6471 *(for men and couples)*

• Conestoga Retreat, 891 Crooked Lane, Ephrata, PA 17522; (717) 738-1680 *(for couples)*

• Harmony Haven Home, 6816 60th Avenue, Evart, MI 49631; (231) 734-5925 *(for men)*

• Haven of Hope Retreat, 1156 Sawmill Road, Rocky Comfort, MO 64861; (417) 435-2510 *(for boys)*

• Haven of Rest, 766 Plaza Drive, Annville, PA 17003; (717) 832-3363 *(for women)*

• Hoffnung Heim, 2333 CR 168, Dundee, OH 44624; (330) 893-2526 *(for women)*

• Hope Cottage, 243 Butler Road, Lebanon, PA 17042; (717) 279-2798 *(for couples)*

• Kurtz Homestead, 360 Kurtz Road, Ephrata, PA 17522; (717) 354-4112 *(for young girls)*

• Ray of Hope, 1478 Baker Road, Penn Yan, NY 14527; (315) 531-8083 *(for girls)*

• Red Rock Refuge, 419 Red Rock Road, Loysville, PA 17047; (717) 536-0021 *(for young boys)*

• Shepherd's Pathway, 1819 McDowell Road, Greencastle, PA 17225; (717) 753-4043 *(for children)*

• Shepherd's Fold, 1820 Quarry Road, Lebanon, PA 17046; (717) 865-3395 *(for men)*

• Still Waters, W7863 Willow Road, Thorpe, WI 54771; (715) 669-5030 *(for women)*

• Sunlight Gardens, 643 Horseshoe Pike, Lebanon, PA 17042; (717) 867-4240 *(for women)*

• Sunrise Meadows, 24 Meadow Lane, Paradise, PA 17562; (717) 687-3700 *(for men)*

• Whispering Hope, 21 Pine Road, Newville, PA 17241; (717) 776-5157 *(for men)*

Church Appointed Crisis Teams:

• Conservative Crisis Intervention, (Mennonite PA); contact: Allen Hoover, 263 Kurtz Road, Ephrata, PA 17522; (717) 354-8508

• Conservative Crisis Intervention, (Amish PA); contact: Amos Stoltzfoos, 3774 East Newport Road, Gordonville, PA 17529; (717) 768-7291

• Conservative Crisis Intervention, (Mennonite NY); contact: Eugene Hoover, 5026 John Greene Road, Dundee, NY 14837; (607) 243-5370

• Conservative Crisis Intervention, (Mennonite WI); contact: Paul Nolt, W5132 Pine Road, Curtiss, WI 54422; (715) 229-4285

• Restoration Team, (Amish OH); contact: Mark Hochstetler, 4312 CR 145, Sugarcreek, OH 44681; (330) 852-3824

• Restoration Team, (Amish, Northeast OH); contact: Jake Mast, 4533 Wilcox Road, Middlefield, OH 44062; (440) 693-4659

• Family Support Team (Amish, Northern IN); contact: Delbert Miller, 15103 CR 20, Middlebury, IN 46540; (574) 825-1326

• Abuse Awareness Team (Amish, Berne, IN); contact: Lovon Hilty, 2900 South 200 West, Berne, IN 46711; (260) 589-2241

• Abuse Awareness Team (Amish, Allen County IN); contact: Lester Schmucker, 11029 SR 101, Harlan, IN 46743; (260) 415-8000

• Family Support Team (Amish, IL); contact: Allen Schrock, 61 North CR 450 East, Arcola, IL 61910; (844)999-3897

• Bloomfield Crisis Connection (Amish, IA); contact: Sam Schrock, 16366 240th Street, Bloomfield, IA 52537; (641) 664-0200

Other recommended resources:
• *Dove's Nest,* 5723 North 99th Street, Omaha, NE 68134; (402) 577-0866
• *Circle of Grace* curriculum, Dove's Nest: (402) 577-0866

About the Authors

Allen Hoover

Allen Hoover owns a small family business, a repair and rebuilding shop, in Ephrata, Pennsylvania. He is part of a church appointed committee, Conservative Crisis Intervention (CCI), which works with abuse cases within the Old Order Mennonite and Amish communities of Pennsylvania, and he has given presentations on preventing abuse in numerous communities and venues. Together with the Old Order Mennonite and Amish School Committees of Pennsylvania they have developed a program for abuse prevention training for teachers that is accepted by the Pennsylvania officials in lieu of the mandated State training. Allen is a member of the Old Order Mennonite Church, Groffdale Conference. He and his wife Rachel live in Ephrata, Pennsylvania. They have eight children and six grandchildren. He can be reached at (717) 354-8508, 263 Kurtz Road, Ephrata, PA 17522.

Dr. Jeanette Harder

Dr. Jeanette Harder is a social work professor at the University of Nebraska at Omaha. She is a co-founder and board member of Dove's Nest: Faith Communities Keeping Children and Youth Safe, and provides cultural awareness trainings for child protection agencies across the United States in areas where there are Plain communities. As the author of *Let the Children Come: Preparing Faith Communities to End Child Abuse and Neglect*, Jeanette cares deeply about the prevention of child abuse in faith communities. Jeanette earned a B.S. from Grace College of the Bible in Omaha, Nebraska, and an MSW and Ph.D. in Social Work from the University of Texas at Arlington. Jeanette and her husband, Stan, are members of First Mennonite Church in Lincoln, Nebraska and have one adult son. She can be reached through Dove's Nest or jeanette@harder.net.